BARBARIC VITALISM

BY

BARBARIC DISCIPLE

BARBARIC VITALISM

Published by RESAVAGER Media

RESAVAGER.COM

© 2023

Table of Contents

FOREWARD

Do you have a moment to talk about Barbaric Vitalism?

The country we live in now is best described as a joke. A clown world. What's up is really down here in the USA. It's Nietzsche's transvaluation of values in real time. A laundry list can be made about all the things wrong with America, but that's all it'd be — a laundry list. The biggest program facing men like us isn't the countless immigrants crossing over. Sure, it's a problem(they all must go back) but not THE problem. The problem is within our ranks, our own citizenry, and even our own families. The problem is internal. At least half of the founding stock populace is convinced national suicide is the morally right course of action and this same half of the population is supported by every institutional power.

You can get mad and yell. You can point to principles or morals, but you can't change the direction the country is headed. In all reality, if you cared at all about the "American way of life" you're already a barbarian in your own country. It's time you start acting like one.

BECOME BARBARIAN

This isn't the obvious conclusion to reach given the circumstances. The barbarians are supposed to be the illegals crossing the border, amirite? No, those people are protected by woke culture and by extension, the regime. You're already a barbarian in their eyes. You're already in enemy territory. The left has shown time and time again it only responds to power — not principle.

It's time you start imagining yourself a barbarian in the true meaning of the term. A barbarian is an outsider, a man who practices foreign traditions and rites. He's not understood or even considered civilized by the society he interacts with. But do you even want to be seen as civilized by this clown world? A barbarian is the sullen eyed Conan with his wolffish instincts and hardness. His eyes dead set on the throne of Aquilonia. He is an usurper. The shining example of Barbaric Vitalism, but Barbaric Vitalism isn't just found in some fictional character.

We remember Rome as the mighty empire the United States modeled itself after. But little talked about is how Rome was founded by a gang of barbarians. The first Romans were men without a city or women of their own. They had to steal the women from neighboring villages with cunning and ruthlessness to continue their bloodlines. Hardly a noble founding by today's "moral" standards. The men of the early Roman Republic exemplified Barbaric Vitalism. Their definition of virtue (virtus) was manliness. Virtue didn't carry the connotations it does today. It just meant you were manly. The way to show your manliness to the Romans was through labor. Strenuous exertions and ordeals made or broke men. In Rome, you weren't born a man. You had to become one.

Manliness — VIRTUE — to the early Romans was associated with physical power, vigor, vitality, energy, and violent action. The Romans compared to the many tribes that surrounded them weren't that impressive. Their adversaries were often bigger, stronger, and outnumbered them. You'd think the way we're taught about the Romans, they won most of their battles, but they actually lost most of them. The Romans were known for their no surrender, never say die mentality. The Romans refused to admit defeat. They lost 50,000 men at Cannae at the hands of Hannibal, but still refused to throw in the towel. The Romans showed energy, vigor, VITALITY. They had the powerful desire to OVERCOME, against all odds. They would rather be killed off than live the rest of their lives as slaves. This is Barbaric Vitalism.

Barbaric Vitalism is a state of mind you reach when you can see nature in its purest form. It's understanding the meaning of life as Nietzsche did, "Life is an instinct for growth, for survival, for the accumulation of forces, for power." Barbaric Vitalism is the powerful zeal for life. It's the feeling Conan must have felt as he strangled the life out of the tyrannical king of Aquilonia on the steps of his throne. Barbaric Vitalism is seeing nature at play and realizing all the bullshit feelings of the modern world don't matter. It's realizing nature doesn't care about equality, decency, or who was where first — nature only cares about who wins.

Barbaric Vitalism is realizing you are a barbarian in your own homeland. You can't just be the noble lion or wolf; you must also play the part of the fox. Become tough and ruthless, but also cunning. Barbaric Vitalism is physical culture. It's becoming the living embodiment power and winning. While the masses spend their time getting fatter and more dependent on the system, free yourself from their control. Refuse their values. Stop caring about what happens to them. They're not your people.

The easiest thing you can do to awaken Barbaric Vitalism is get stronger. The Ancient Greeks understood the importance of strength and power which is why they banned slaves from training in the gymnasium. The masters who rule over us try to do the same, but through deception, not force. They want you to choose comfort and safety over strength and suffering. They want you to believe strength comes at the cost of intellect, when in fact, it enhances it. Barbarians wouldn't let themselves be dominated like Americans are today. They would have the courage to say no and push back. They would stand and fight. This kind of man doesn't just rise to the occasion, his life is already struggle. He's prepared himself for the fight. His mettle already tested. This — for him — is just another challenge, another ordeal to overcome. You too, must embrace the struggle.

Any man who dedicates himself to physical culture becomes changed. Training teaches man to overcome, to test his mettle, to go to war. It takes just one achievement, one reached goal in the gym to reveal the power of Barbaric Vitalism and see the world as it's meant to be seen.

PART ONE:
I WILL TEACH AMERICANS A LESSON
THEY WILL REMEMBER IN THEIR BONES

1.

I will teach Americans a lesson they will remember in their bones.

It is a hard lesson to hear, but it must be heard. Americans — and I should be specific when saying Americans — are a people removed from their heritage in a way they don't understand the ramifications thereof. When I say Americans, I mean White people of European origins whose ancestors migrated to America before the War Between the States. Now this American blood of yours may have some combination of the European tribes. It may matter whether your bloodline comes more from the North or South, but for our purposes, it matters little. Americans underwent ethnogenesis on the frontier. We became something apart from our European cousins.

We are our own people. You are only a part of this group if you're able to trace your family lines back to before the War Between the States and more preferably, the War for Independence. It makes little difference if you trace it from your father's or your mother's side, though you should always most identify with your father's lineage. You can still identify with your European cousins, we share the same fight for survival, but you are distinct. Just recognize that our goals are not one, but we may be allies here and now.

What are the ramifications of my definition of American? What about all those other people who came to this country after the War Between the States? "How can a man be so racist?" might be a leftist response to what I've just said. Listen well: you've been indoctrinated into a worldview that dispossesses you from your birthright. Dispossesses you from everything your ancestors accomplished in the name of your bloodline. Who are you to betray your own blood over the propaganda of the enemy? How can you apply today's values to men who lived two hundred years ago? I thought you were supposed to be the more scientific, more progressive, more understanding, and tolerant in comparison to these "horrible" people that lived hundreds of years ago. Where is your education?

No — if your ancestors came to this country after the Civil War, you aren't American by blood. If you refer to yourself as a HYPHENATED American, you are not American by blood. If you attack the 2nd Amendment, you are not American by blood. You don't even have to describe what an American looks like. The world knows what an American looks like. Now, I'm not here to hold ill will to the millions of pretenders and foreigners residing in this country now. They did what anyone else would do. Our "leaders" sold out the country and betrayed its founding stock. Now you may come to me and say you are American, but I would require you to prove it. Prove your loyalty to our tribe. Would you denounce your hyphenation, your ethnic heritage, just to be an American? If you're willing to do this, I'm willing to accept you in our ranks as a man of RACE.

What of the American way and Americanism? The whole idea of the melting pot? "American is an idea." "We are a country of immigrants." America is not an idea. America is a country with well-defined borders. We are not a country of immigrants, we are a country of settlers, frontiersmen, and conquerors. This was not an empty land for the taking, our ancestors had to fight for it.

"What about the crimes against the Indians," one might wail. What are you still doing here if you cared about the crimes against the Indians? What of the Indian brutality? War is a part of life and nature. It's something that comes like the seasons. No one will put an end to war. To think your progressive ideology has any chance of that is to be naïve. You have been mindfucked by the people you trusted to show you how to live.

2.
"In a multiethnic polity, ethnic politics take precedence over everything else." -Lee Kuan Yew

America has become a multiethnic country, there is no denying this. Many talk about returning to some kind of civic nationalism we had before the civil rights act, but there will be no returning. The universe cannot go back in time. There is only one way and that is forward. Whether you understand and prepare for this is another thing entirely. If you do not, history will continue without you. The civil rights act doesn't exist to create the dream of equality and liberal democracy, it exists SOLELY to hold down the rightful heirs to the country.

It's a means of taking power from the blood that founded this country. Consolidating that power at the top, along with heaps of wealth, and letting the masses fight over the crumbs. And in this fight, the whole might of the government apparatus is charged only with going after the rightful heirs to the land. We have entered into a battle that was lost before we were even born, with both arms tied behind our backs. But the war still rages. As long as we still breathe, the war will rage on.

Ethnic politics overtook the civic nationalism of the past. Americans have become the "great evil" in this country, responsible for all the shortcomings of others. The state is used to enforce the concept of equity. To bring up the "marginalized" peoples to the height of the White Man. They've had almost as much time to do this as it took our ancestors to spread from the thirteen colonies to the Pacific Coast. Have they solved racism and inequality? Have they solved anything?

No, ethnic strife is higher than it's ever been. The state has only accomplished what it set out to do: dispossess Americans and mobilize millions of foreigners against the founding stock. They don't believe in equity or democracy, only the saps they mindfuck care about that. These people only care about money and power. Divide and conquer is their way. It's what the Romans did after all. Get the barbarians to eat each other.

How far has America fallen from the 1960s? We had our sights set on the STARS. We put men on the moon. The next frontier was in our sights. And what now? What's most important now is we sit our asses down and listen to some overweight black woman talk about how she's oppressed in her fully paid scholarship to some university. We don't talk about the stars anymore, only how EVIL the poor Whites who shop at Walmart are. How they are single-handedly holding back the paradise of liberal democracy.

The only people trying to make this multiethnic empire work are over "educated," liberal Americans. All the other races know what the game is. They see what Lee Kuan Yew did in Singapore. It's only natural. Yes, it is very natural for humans to act in their self-interests. Their interests are united with those of the tribe they come out of. What you'll find in the foreigners who come to our country is they self-segregate into their own neighborhoods. Look at somewhere like Los Angeles: you have Chinatown, Armenia town, etcetera,

etcetera. It's not something I fault anyone for, they're doing what it takes to survive. My job is to get my people to do the same. To get us back on the path.

Liberal progressives will offer multitudes of excuses for this and find a way to blame it on the dreaded boogeyman, White supremacy. What these foreigners are doing, however, is surviving. They're sticking together. Using the system that already works for them, the rigged system, to set up their own little communities in the United States. It's something our own still do where they can. Genetically, we're more likely to trust someone of the same race and language. Race is an extension of kin. Don't believe the lies that race is only skin deep, that it's unimportant. Race is DIVINE.

You can't change how you were born. You are what you are. Much had to happen to make you possible. Your bloodline stretches back to the beginning of mankind. Do you have any understanding of this? The color of your skin comes from where your people migrated from. How they adapted to the environment. The full differences between the races are likely known but covered up by the greedy and the corrupt trying to profit off us all. The most important thing to remember is that we evolved differently and SEPARATELY.

The genes do mix. There is no master race or anything like that, but the races are NOT equal. Sometimes it is WAR that creates mixing. For Americans, it was the expansion into the frontier. This is how you get ethnogenesis. The groups involved in ethnogenesis are engaged in the true struggle: the fight for survival. Each race is suited to its own path. This path is defined by their valuation of good and bad. It is my hope to get you onto The Golden Path. This Golden Path isn't something shared by Americans alone, but by all who wish for the survival of the species.

3.

People are best served by having strong racial cohesion. This is something difficult for the American, raised on the myth of the melting pot and individualism, to understand. To think beyond it is heresy, but you must because the myth of the melting pot spells the end of us all. If you don't advocate for yourself and your people, no one will. Never, never forget this. It ain't about hating other races, it's about taking care of your own.

The failure of this leads to all the problems America is suffering through now. Our county was 90% White until the civil rights act. The latest census in 2020 has us down to 58% of the population. What do you call that? Has becoming a multiethnic empire made us better? Stronger? Has it made your life easier? Has it made you a better person? Compare the average American in the 1960s to the average American today.

Are we stronger? Healthier? Do we know more than our ancestors did? Are we better than our ancestors? Or have we just been made sick by this society? Dragged away from gazing at the stars and back into the weeds of anti-White hatred. How many have been made so sick and deranged by the state that they've turned against their own race? How many have been so mindfucked that they think they were born into the wrong body? How many have forgotten that they are PHYSICAL as well as mental beings?

The people of color you claim share in your multiethnic "identify" are grifting at the expense of you and all True Americans. If you examine their lives, you'll find that it doesn't resemble the life you are choosing. You'll find that they have prejudices, and they maintain their separate cultural identities. It's only the educated liberal who has abandoned his own. Is this person a TRAITOR to his blood? I want to believe them only mindfucked, but if being shown the truth isn't enough to turn them back on the path, they are indeed, traitors. The real traitors, however, are the ones who put these changes in the country into motion and the ones who perpetuate it for their benefit at the expense of the tribe.

4.

It is said that the path we're on now is the natural course of the liberal democracy established in the founding of the United States. And this may be true. Many Americans put a lot of faith in the founding of our country, its documents, and the institutions in Washington DC. This is a terrible mistake. Academics like to paint fairytales as to why the colonists rebelled against the British Empire, but the reality was they had always governed themselves. The Revolution was always going to happen. The taxes imposed upon the colonies were measly in comparison to what we deal with today.

It may be that the Constitution of the United States is the greater tyranny. Paper constitutions wield overwhelming social power without conscious, without limitations. The state — as Friedrich Nietzsche proclaimed in his *Thus Spoke Zarathustra* — is the "coldest of all cold monsters." Now I speak of heresy to the red-blooded American conservative, but it must be done. If the "American way" has led us to this point, of what use is it? How much of the "American way" is just an invention of the post-World War II United States? Maybe there are enough strong men to fix our problem, but what's to prevent this from happening down the line long after we are dead?

Not everything in that document is false. Every man should be armed. Every man should be a warrior. Our ability to pick ourselves up by our bootstraps is to be commended. The reality we face today is the Constitution is already subverted and replaced by a new constitution: the civil rights act. It is possible to honor your ancestors, but also learn from their mistakes. This I ask you to do.

5.

What do I propose over this liberal democracy? What do I propose in the place of the "sacred" Constitution? This is the reason I write this book, but before we get into what I propose, I want you to understand that it is not the Constitution or the institutions in Washington that made America great. Many think this is what makes America the best country in the world. No, what made America great was Americans. Americans were the last race to be forced back into nature. We rediscovered our BARBARIC VITALISM and FRONTIER SPIRIT.

The frontier changed us. The frontier made us who we are. It made us distinct from our European cousins. There is much written about this, especially from Europeans encountering Americans during the Great War. Our history is full of men who made their own way. They dealt with their own problems, alone in the woods, with a gun, if necessary. Our blood thrives on the frontier. I'd wager many people's blood thrives on the frontier.

You must remember what you've been conditioned to forget. Our bodies are the result of hundreds of thousands of years of adaptation. Our species is known for its conquest and mastery of new space. This continued until mankind became the dominant species on the planet. There is something you learn when you start to break leftist mental conditioning and do simple things such as exercise or eat healthily. You learn it when you go on a hike or any experience in nature. The body responds well to stress. It's almost as if stress itself is vitality.

Physical stress is vigor to the human body. It's an act of war and war is a force that calls you back to life. When you take the most basic act of taking care of yourself, in earnest, your entire worldview begins to change. You start to realize that society is lying and if they're lying to you about something like nutrition, or women, you have to ask, what else are they lying to you about? This world they've set up for us is soft, it's made us lose our edge. It's making us lose what it means to be human. You can't look at the exemplars of liberal democracy and tell me they are the exemplars of what it means to be human.

I encourage you to again, be human. To venture out into the frontier in the spirit of adventure. At the very least, take the basic steps of taking care of yourself. Make yourself strong and eat right. What do you risk by this, beyond making yourself better able to take care of your family? What they offer you isn't human. It's slavery of the cruelest sort. They want to take everything that makes us American and turn us into COWS TO BE MILKED.

6.

To be a human is to belong to a race, to a tribe. We have to start thinking like a tribe again. We have to start thinking like a collective again. What matters above all else is the strength and survival of the tribe. Now it is easy to say you don't know these people who I tell you are part of your tribe. Hell, you probably don't like all the people in your own family. According to Pierre van den Berghe, RACE is an extension of kin. He also believed that ethnicity is the driver of a people.

Van den Berghe also noted that people trusted their own more so than foreigners, even when it came to tyrannies. They would rather be unjustly ruled by their own than be unjustly ruled by someone of a different race. I am just a man. I don't come from any noble house or lineage. I've worked a normal job all my life. My experience parrots what van den Berghe observed in his studies. You must understand that races don't do this out of hate, they do it out of a survival instinct to master space.

Liberals talk about how we've moved past these racist survival instincts. The truth is almost every race — except Americans — still operates under them. Again, not out of hate of other races, they just don't trust other races as easily as they trust members of their own race in the same way you wouldn't trust a stranger over your own family. It could be something as innocent as they don't speak the language and feel like they won't get swindled by working only with someone who speaks their tongue. It could very well be malicious. What's important to remember is it still happens and it is still the standard. Something I like to add is that the American tendency to ignore his survival instinct may very be an example of that very same survival instinct, as the American is trusting in the institutions created by his ancestors, believing those institutions will always do right by him.

You only have one way out of this mess, and it starts by becoming a race again. By looking out for your own, above all else. You might think you don't have anything in common with them, but if you try it, you'll find trust comes much easier to your own race than those of other races. Especially in today's world where we all face the same dangers to our livelihood. We all see the game being played against us. Those who have betrayed us see the game as means of conquering Americans and those who haven't betrayed the blood understand the game out of the instinct to survive and overcome, against all odds.

You have to start creating links in the chain. Form relationships with your people. Brotherhoods with your closest friends that get passed down to your sons and his sons. The brotherhood of armed men is the foundation of a people. Every man a warrior. This is the goal you should set your sights on. It's something you must do. Our species is in dire straits.

7.

We've stagnated as a species. It's folly to have all our eggs in one basket. Mankind must expand into the stars. The moment you stray too far from natural law, nature begins to sow the seeds of your destruction. It is known that Earth won't be around forever, yet you see our "sophisticated and intelligent" society moving toward measures to save the planet through implementing "green technology" instead of developing a way to move beyond the Earth. How much further into space could we have gotten had we continued down the path?

The lesson Americans need to remember in their bones is this: stagnation equals death. We evolved to go out into the unknown and master space, master the conditionings we are born into. Our bodies are tougher than we realize. We have to go out and conquer. To not test our limits is a death sentence to the species. Maybe it's not your problem. The end is a long way off after all — but you owe a duty to the blood.

The only reason you're here is generations upon generations of your ancestors finding a way, no matter how hard the times were, to secure the future for their descendants. There is no greater crime than ending a bloodline because you're somehow ashamed of your people's history — a history that's been maligned by very bad people in order to get you to quit, to give up. You are the steward of your bloodline while you breathe. I don't care who you are, you owe a duty to your blood. The good news in all this is we have time. The world isn't going to end tomorrow. There is still time to redeem your parents and grandparents.

The most powerful way to get Americans back on the path is religion, but not just any religion, a WARRIOR RELIGION. Lucky for the American, strength and fighting is in our blood. And we will have to fight. What I will introduce to you in this book is nothing foreign, nothing that the True American couldn't understand.

8.

Strive for Superiority.

When you look at ancient examples of WARRIOR RELIGIONS like Sparta, you see their Lawgiver, Lycurgus, forging a people based on excellence and virtue, and you get a city-state that reigned for 800 years. Compare this to modern democracies like the United States where the wheels have come off after a couple hundred years. Yes, it's supposed to be a Republic, but we all know how our enemies like to use this word, "liberal democracy." To govern and reign in the right way gives a government the Mandate of Heaven. Our country used to have this Mandate when there was a vast frontier before us. Our men warlike, our women powerful mothers pushing out 6, 8, 12, 14 kids in their lifetimes(and they talk to us about how we cannot sustain birth rates so we must import third world). Our people were able to populate and conquer this country from a few settlements on the eastern coast.

The enemy wants Americans to feel bad about our history. But how can you when it's filled with so much greatness? Jonathan Bowden once said that 98% of history that's of importance was realized by dead White European males. This will always be a White Man's world, even now, the enemy rides the coattails of the White Man's greatness. While you've been having a pity party about supposed crimes your ancestors committed against poor poc, you've let those "marginalized" groups take over. Can you show me what good they've done with that power? How have they changed the world? How have they turned the wheel of mankind?

We were traveling to the moon at the height of our power when we turned the reins over to diversity. What have they done to push us further into the future? All that's been wrought is the civilizational decline and the promise of race wars. Competency in almost every area of life has gone down the toilet, from the movies coming out of Hollywood to our ability to count the votes of an election to our military's ability to fly a helicopter. As a society, we went from California refusing to legalize gay marriage in 2008 to taking our kids to drag queen story hour at the local library and performing gender-change surgeries on children in 2022. We've allowed for almost everything and the quality of man has declined as a result. We have fewer friends, fewer skills, and more mental illness and disease.

They've had every chance to show us how diversity is superior. How it makes us stronger. And what have they done with this chance? They've turned into a game of blame Whitey for their own incompetence. Our people gave them the chance to show the superiority of their ways and what have they done beyond playing this blame game? What, we didn't give diversity enough time? The American settler reached the Pacific coast within a hundred years of the founding of the country. California was incorporated in 1850, some seventy-four years after 1776. What have they done in the same amount of time to make America greater?

The result of around sixty years of civil rights is an American population who's had their pride and exceptionalism swept out from under them. Their 90% of the population down to 58%, creating skyrocketing inflation and less opportunity for the descendants of the great people who conquered the New World. Now you shouldn't cry "woe to me," any more than you should try and claim victimhood as your enemy has. What's done is done, there's no turning back the clock. Much has been taken, yes, but you have a chance to prove your worth to the world. To prove the strength of your BLOOD. This wretched complacency we've been seduced by must end.

9.

"Whatever maketh them rule and conquer and shine, to the dismay and envy of their neighbours, they regard as the high and foremost thing, the test and the meaning of all else." -
Friedrich Nietzsche

What's been plaguing the American is the inability to move effectively against the left. Yes, our enemies hold all the keys to all the doors, this is true. It goes further than that, however: our people don't believe in themselves anymore. Many have bought into this fake White guilt. Many more are just afraid of being called racist. Those who have managed to identify good and bad, who your friends are and who your enemies are, don't know how to move the bar forward. What's effective versus what's not.

This problem comes down primarily to being plugged into the old value system. The American value system of our ancestors is outdated, and our enemies use it against us. Most attacks aimed at the enemy are likened to a spirited debate between fellow countrymen, whereas the left treats Americans like they're a blight upon this earth, devils from hell to be vanquished. There's no bottom to how low they'll go to win. Everything is on the table, and they dream of the day they have you raped and murdered. So first and foremost, stop looking at these people as your countrymen. You're born into an eternal war for survival, one that's been going on long before you were born and likely continue long after you die.

The belief structures of our people are in shambles. They don't have confidence in who they are. They don't believe — as their ancestors did — that they were better and exceptional, that they had divine providence. This is why I compared the conquest of the frontier to the leftist reign of civil rights. How much was really accomplished by diversity? They couldn't do a thing which is why everything turned to "first black woman this" or "first lgbt that." We're celebrating not the excellence of the American frontier spirit, but which "marginalized" person can accomplish what the White Man already pioneered long before them — and this is after we help them with policies like affirmative action and the lowering of standards.

Bronze Age Pervert has it right when we push actions like bodybuilding, eating right, or reading old books. These things rebuild the confidence of men who got a rotten deal in their youth through public education. One goal is to push these men toward fighting, surviving, and strength — the watchwords of martial peoples. This is a good path. Through anonymity, people are learning how to fight back. Where we want to go next, to truly move the bar, is establishing good and bad.

Everything your enemy does is bad. Everything your side does is good. This seems almost childish but let me tell you a little-known story about the hero, Herakles. Long before he was known as Herakles — a name he took on by suggestion of the Oracle at Delphi to stave off the rage of White-Armed Hera — he lived in Thebes, which owed a debt to a nearby people called the Minyans. When the Minyan heralds came to collect the yearly debt, Herakles "subjected them to shameful mutilation." He cut off their ears, noses, and hands, and strung them all up into necklaces which he put around their necks before sending them all back packing, empty-handed, to their king.

This caused another war between the Thebans and Minyans, but this time, the Thebans had Herakles on their side. He won the battle and made the Minyans take on the same debt but double the amount and term. This gives keen insights into the nature of the Greks in general. They saw the debt levied against the Thebans as unjust and the debt levied against the Minyans after their defeat as just. This is something the American has a hard time understanding because you're indoctrinated into this pseudo-leftist/Christian ideology. But it's not complicated, bad things happen to the enemy equals

23

good, and bad things that happen to us are bad. The hypocritical bullshit you see coming out of leftists today would be understood by the Ancient Greks as right and just.

10.

"Much that passed for good with one people was regarded with scorn and contempt by another: thus I found it." - Friedrich Nietzsche

The transvaluation of all values is a subject talked about at length by Nietzsche. It was underway in his time and damn near completed in our own. This is how the leftist gained power, by redefining good and bad. There lies the path for the American to fight back. You must again start this process of reevaluating all values but through the lenses of an American Vitalist.

The values of one neighboring people are almost opposite to those of the other. If you want to gain ground, you must make others buy into our value system. To make bad everything that belongs to the enemy and make good everything that belongs to us. Once you can do this and make your disciples fanatical in their ways, you will be ready for a fight. There is no negotiating in this matter. You make good all that is opposite of the enemy. If they value weakness, ugliness, and mental illness, you will value strength, beauty, and intelligence.

There are no half roads, no bridges to be left unburnt. Anything the enemy does is bad because they want to destroy us. Anything we do is good in comparison to the enemy. You see the left use this tactic often and when they can't paint themselves in a good light, they hide or bury the story. This is what it means to have healthy race instincts. You must give power to everything that gives courage to our side and makes us look strong and powerful while making disappear anything bad or from the enemy. What's good and bad solidifies what makes a people and differentiates them from their neighbors.

11.

Real American History

You learn in school that history is written by the victors, but you don't apply that principle to your own country. Americans are made to believe the two most pinnacle events in American history are defeating the Confederacy in the War Between the States to free the slaves and defeating Nazi Germany in the Second World War to save the Jews. We're the good guys — am I right? How do you know that's how history went down? How do you know they're not lying to you? The common response would be: why would they lie? Probably the most convincing part is the teachers themselves, believe what they're telling you.

If you make it to college and beyond, you've shown qualities other than intellectual prowess. You've shown that you're good at taking orders. You've shown that you can comply with the directions given to you. You can be made to be agreeable. Thought that runs against the grain in universities is usually smoked out and excised. Maybe the professors are smart enough to know they're being bullshitted but too afraid to step out of line. They don't want to lose their tenure or be ostracized from their community. Most academics are cowards.

I'm going to introduce you to a more honest view of American history. This thought isn't mine, it belongs primarily to two men. One goes by the pseudonym Thomas777, the other is national treasure, James LaFond. You need to look both of them up if you want a more accurate view of history. Thomas777's focus is primarily on the Second World War and the Cold War while LaFond spent much time researching the true history of slavery in America. Through reading these two men, you have no choice but to conclude that the good guys don't always win. America's "shameful" history goes beyond slavery and racism.

At the beginning of this book, I told you what the two pinnacle moments of the American race were. It wasn't freeing the slaves or saving the Jews. It was the Revolutionary War and War Between the States. If your bloodline appeared in this country before the War Between the States, your ancestors took part in the forging of the United States and you're American by race. What I will talk to you about now is America in a way you didn't hear about in school. Why should you believe these two men over academia? Well, you know the news is fake. Why would history be any different?

Did you know that the original name of the thirteen colonies was the Plantations? Did you also know that blacks were not the only slaves? They were expensive so most Plantation owners opted for White slaves, yes White slaves. They needed labor in the New World and England just happened to be overcrowded. White Men would be made indentured servants to some master. Told if they served for a few years, say seven, they would be made free and given what they needed to start their own farm. The problem was most didn't survive the contract or had their contracts unfairly lengthened. They were run into the ground in hopes that they would die, and the master wouldn't have to pay them out at the end. Minor aggressions and breaches of the contract allowed the masters to take on more years on the servant's contract.

Ok—these people signed up for it, so what? Well, the need for labor kept growing. They needed bodies, so the slave traders went as far as to kidnap English children and ship them to the New World. After the Civil War, you can understand why we stopped referring to America as the Plantations. James LaFond has written many books on the subject including direct evidence for these claims in the form of masters writing advertisements for the local papers, trying to find their lost

26

White slaves, and English families petitioning for the return of their kidnapped children. Another misconception is that the American colonists were brutally persecuted by the British Empire using heavy taxes, but when you look at the taxes they were forced to pay, you have to ask why WE haven't overthrown the United States government by now. In comparison, the taxes imposed on the colonists were measly compared to what we put up with today.

The only perspective you get on the War for Independence is from the colonists themselves. Maybe you should try reading something from a loyalist perspective. There is a book called *The True History of the American Revolution* by Sydney George Fisher that examines the conflict from both sides, actually talking about the war from the British perspective. What Fisher discovered was the colonists weren't as oppressed as your history teacher wants you to believe. What was happening in America during the time of the Revolution was the emergence of a new elite. This elite had come into being thanks to the British Empire's hands-off approach to the New World. For the most part, they didn't charge taxes, they let the local senators in the colonies determine the salaries of the governors the Empire sent to rule. All trade was supposed to go through the British fleet, but colonists regularly went around this and took their own shipments from Europe.

By the time of the Revolution, England was hurting for money. Its people were heavily taxed, so they decided to charge the Plantations for some of the services they rendered, such as war debt for defending them during the French and Indian War. Now this isn't some argument that the British did nothing wrong and we should have never split. Put aside the new rising American elite and just focus on the people themselves. Most Americans weren't seduced by the liberal thought of the time coming from thinkers like Locke. The only book most Americans read, if they read anything at all, was the Bible. Why then, did they fight the British Empire?

Americans, via the British Empire's hands-off approach, had grown accustomed to governing themselves. They had always done things on their own. They made the Plantations self-sustaining and as Fisher says in his book, the Revolution was always going to happen, even if there wasn't a Tea Tax. The vitality of life on the frontier was already changing what was in the blood of the colonists. Bringing out qualities not seen in hundreds of years. They would not be ruled by anyone but themselves.

12.

Let's move from the Revolution to the War Between the States. In history class, it's called the American Civil War, but that's its name post-propaganda. I will use a more neutral War Between the States, if you were more southern in your inclinations, you might call it the War of Northern Aggression. Most Americans believe this war was fought to free the slaves, but the reality is the slaves were an afterthought. Take President Lincoln himself who is on record of saying many interesting things. He said if he could preserve the Union without freeing the slaves, he would have done so. He also contemplated sending all the Africans back to Africa, not believing the two races could live side by side. Did you also know that Lincoln wanted Robert E Lee to lead the Union forces and there was an attempt made to get him to do? How does this make you feel?

If you look back to the times, you realize that the anti-slavery Americans of the time weren't so different from the leftists today. I recommend a book called *A Disease of the Public Mind* by Thomas Fleming, if interested in learning more about this. Freeing the slaves didn't come until the final year of the war. Rather, the war was fought over state's rights.

13.

In the aftermath of the War Between the States, the South went under reconstruction to reincorporate it back into the Union. You should note that today we are talking about tearing down Confederate statues and renaming military bases, but Union soldiers and Confederates didn't feel that way during the time. There was much respect between the two sides. Some of the Generals and warriors we honor from the American military during the Second World War looked up to men like Robert E Lee and Thomas "Stonewall" Jackson. During Reconstruction, the South was invaded by northern "carpetbaggers" who were exploiting the Southerners. This practice led to the creation of another infamous group: the KKK. The KKK is known today only by what it became after Reconstruction, but its original purpose was much different. They were a response to the carpetbaggers and acted as a shield for a vulnerable population.

14.

Everyone wants to trace leftism back to its point of origin in the belief that if they can find it, they will have the knowledge they need to finally defeat the enemy. For America, this was 1933 when the communists infiltrated the Roosevelt administration and academia in general. Do what you will with this information.

Read *American Betrayal* by Diana West, if interested in learning more.

15.

The Second World War is seen by most Americans as the moment America saved the world and became a superpower on the world stage. We were grievously attacked at Pearl Harbor(we didn't do nuffin) and declared war on the Axis powers. Every leftist has wet dreams about the Second World War. To get that one chance to punch a real Nazi in the face at Normandy. To be on that beach, man.

Well, let's take another look at how it all went down. We like to see Nazi Germany as the Great Satan of our modern world. Nazis are like Christian demons, wanting to exterminate anything that isn't Aryan. What historians leave out, however, is very important facts and information as to WHY Germany went hot for fascism in the 1930s. The end of the First World War was bitter for the Germans. They had to face off against the world to honor their alliance with the Austro-Hungarian Empire. During the most brutal war to ever occur at the time, involving conditions no man would ever want to be in, the German army was never pushed back behind German borders. They fought valiantly. The Great War produced a Warrior I will reference much in this book: Ernst Jünger. He is the exemplar of what we would consider a Western samurai, or as close to a samurai as we would get when you contrast our different values.

Germany had to throw in the towel, and they did so after a peace proposal offered by none other than Woodrow Wilson, the President of the United States at the time. Germany was under the impression that they would get the terms that Wilson offered them, but the Allies chose NOT to honor that deal. France wanted retribution. They wanted Germany to pay for the entire war. And they were made to. The interwar years are something you don't learn about in school. It was a time of great turmoil for a broken Germany. There was strife between fascists and communists. The country itself was handed over to communists after the war.

What happened in that time? Germany became broke, all its revenue being shipped to the Allies. Communists took control with the aid of countries like England. Degeneracy became rampant. Leftists like to talk about how the Nazis burned books, but did you ever ask what books they were burning? They were books on trannies, pedos, gays, and the like, stuff parents didn't want around their kids. Germany was going through its own "woke" period.

What do you know, the degeneration into a tranny state led to the rise of Hitler. What does that mean for our society? Is the next Hitler around the corner? Perhaps, he is one of you. But to get back to the Second World War, it's said to have started when Germany invaded Poland. France and England were forced to respond, but what they don't tell you is Soviet Russia also invaded Poland. How come war wasn't declared on Russia?

Another "crime" of the Nazis was the holocaust or the slaughter of six million Jews — or was it four million? They're never concrete on the number. Let's not get into the discussion about the gas chambers. Now Americans are appalled by this. Many red-blooded Americans believe they have to check their own self-interests because if they advocated for themselves, they might become like the Nazis. Four million is a lot of people, but I ask you, WHY do we care about this slaughter of Jews and not the killing of the ten to twenty million Russians by the Soviets before a shot was fired in World War II? What makes the poor Jews more important than the Russians who died before the holocaust?

What you have to understand is the holocaust, if it was carried out the way they say, was not done out of the blue out of some meaningless racism. Germans saw what was happening on their eastern frontier. They saw the massacre of millions of Russians by the Soviets. You see the Soviets kill ten million and then invade Poland, what are you going to start thinking? You're going to start thinking that if the communists take Poland, well, who's next? To condemn one tragedy and not the other is intellectual dishonesty. This wasn't some evil act by a madman, but the fight for survival.

Now to return to America and the "unprovoked" attack on Pearl Harbor by the Japanese. The reality was the United States government wanted in the war, but the American public did not. Communists had been the administration since 1933. They were already sending arms and supplies to the Soviet Union. They just needed some excuse and that came in the form of Japan which allied itself with Germany. In response, the United States started choking off the resources going to Japan. By the time of Pearl Harbor, the Japanese saw the strike as their one chance to break free. If it failed(it did as the carrier fleet was away from the base at the time, again, the US knew the attack was coming), it wouldn't be long until the Japanese ran out of resources.

Patton himself at the end of the war recognized the game being played and commented that we had defeated the wrong enemy. But by then, it was already too late. To recap, Germany saw a very real threat in Soviet Russia and was responding to that threat as best it could. I did not mention the Nazis pulled off one of the greatest economic recoveries in history to launch the Second World War, bringing England and France to their knees in the process. America, the supposed good guys in the Second World War, were directly supplying a Soviet regime that has massacred millions of people before the war even began. Is it no surprise why there was so much American support for Germany at the beginning of the war? If this seems like a lot, let's see if I can make it easier to understand. Let's bring it back to Hollywood movies.

In 2008, there was a fun(but ridiculous) action movie made called *Wanted* starring James McAvoy. The premise of the movie is this nerd realizes he's the son of a deadly assassin and he's inherited his father's genes, making him capable of being just as deadly. Now, this movie was based on a comic book series of the same name. The movie dropped the original premise of the comic book which I thought was more interesting than the one presented in the film. In the comic book, the protagonist is the son of a supervillain, and he comes to learn that in his world, the supervillains won, killing off all the superheroes. This is a better interpretation to take towards recent history. You live in a world made of globalist gangsters, not heroes. History is always written by the victors, to justify their actions, and make them look like the heroes in history.

Nazi Germany, through the Nuremberg Trials, was made out to be carrying a "criminal" war against the world and ruthlessly persecuting the Jews. Before the Second World War, there was a different conception of war. It was something that came like the seasons. How do you criminalize the Nazi actions in the Second World War, but not the American firebombings of German cities or the dropping of nuclear warheads on Japan? This is Victor's justice. The Nuremberg Trials were a sham. They struggled to find a judge that would even preside over it. You look up Thomas777 if interested in learning more about this.

16.

Civil rights is another marred moment in American history. The civil rights act itself became the new defacto constitution of the United States as it overruled the original document in every case where they met. Most notably gone is the FREEDOM OF ASSOCIATION. We like to look back at the opponents of civil rights as evil White racists, but if you look at a book named *The Age of Entitlement* by Christopher Caldwell. You find at the time two opposing mindsets. The opponents of civil rights thought things were changing too fast and the proponents thought it was changing too slowly. Integration was done by the point of a gun by the US military, not by choice.

You have to realize we lost something from the civil rights era. We used to be a people, with a sense of racial cohesion and unity. We used to know who we are. Some people would call

33

this White racialism, but it was something that was just part of the human condition. All races practiced nepotism. Yes, this is nepotism, not racism. All races favored their own over others, and you see it still today. Blacks for example, always rally behind their own in any manufactured racial conflict, no matter how much of a scumbag the guy ends up being.

Americans of the time were practicing their natural instincts. They weren't evil. They were RIGHTFULLY trying to take care of their own and history as shown them to be just in their actions. Look at what's become of us.

17.

You must remember that this information doesn't change the game. It's been known. You won't convince anyone of it unless they're ready to be convinced. I include it to make you more FANATICAL for your cause, to know that you're fighting for the truth. The sacred liberal democracy they keep warning you is always in danger and must be secured is nothing but a cover for a gangster ruling class to stay out of the limelight.

18.

Kin and Country

Something not talked about enough is the devastation of the family in our "liberal democracy." Maybe I feel the devastation more keenly because my family stayed in California when so many others left for greener pastures. The importance of family, however, supersedes everything else. As a kid, you see the world through rose-colored goggles and don't always see the problems in your own family, but for me, I only remember the decline. And then, when my father passed away, the family sort of crumbled away. What happened to my family is just one story of many in America during this time as the great transition from reliance on kin to reliance on the state finally completes.

For most of American history, Americans were capable of being self-reliant. Those on the frontier didn't have to stop by their local grocery store every week for food. They grew their food or hunted or traded with their neighbors. Those in cities learned trades and weren't incapable of going out into nature to survive. Early Americans didn't rely on the mommy state to provide "dem programs." You either found a way to survive or you died off. The metaphysics of this time supported this environment.

Now however, with the massive influx of immigrants, which in turn, makes for less opportunity for the founding stock, we have created the perfect storm for "dem programs." Leftists, of course, will call you racist for this and because the right has caved on the issue, the bloodletting continues. When you think about what the state is trying to accomplish, it helps to think of the leftist movie *V For Vendetta* when the supreme leader guy tells his shadow government: "Make them remember WHY. THEY. NEED. US!" They need Americans to keep shoveling money for them to launder and keep up the grift. On the societal level, families are getting hit hard and breaking down, just trying to stay afloat.

If the average American could be made to see how much was stolen from him, he would chimp out. Not just the money, but the destruction and alienation from the family. The heritage and traditions lost to time. Lessons he didn't get to learn from his parents, aunts and uncles, and grandparents. It's true that many are incapable of seeing this. They're so dependent on(and mindfucked by) the system that they will share its fate. Let's not forget the ones who had the right QUALITY and had that quality squandered by the regime. Think of the brave men killed or maimed in the Middle East just to open the doors for more immigration into the country.

19.

There is a group in America I have much respect for and hopefully, they don't hate me for what I have to say. This group is best described as the love-for-country conservatives. They almost always have a boomer mindset. It's defend America at all costs. You cannot betray America. If you tell them you're leaving for greener pastures and better opportunities for your family, they'll think you're betraying America. You didn't stand and fight. Mike Ma described them as holding onto the mast of a sinking ship while being stabbed by mixed-race teens.

Even if your leaders are corrupt and hostile, you must be patriotic. You must defend America! In some ways, this is a very admirable mindset. You want your people to think like this, but in another way, your "chosen" elite knows how to take advantage of this mentality and use it to destroy Americans. I don't know if they realize this, but if you let the founding stock be wiped out, you don't have the same country. You can honor the American spirit and be patriotic about it, but if you support the regime that's destroying your people no matter what, to what end are your goals? There aren't any successful multi-ethnic democracies in the world.

The greatness of a country comes from the character of its PEOPLE. It goes deeper than patriotism. The civic nationalism found in this love-for-country patriot is misguided. It's often found in veterans because they took an OATH and oaths are powerful things that most on the right don't understand. I too have this love for country but for the real America. Not the nasty tranny state it's become.

I'm certain many on the boomer love-for-country side have suffered much as my own family has suffered. Surely, many found a way to survive and thrive like they were supposed to, but a man like Trump couldn't have been elected if that was the case for the majority. Leftism has separated our people from the heritage and traditions that made us great, made us strong. Its demonized strategies races have used since the beginning of time to survive and thrive. The reason states like Russia and China can have so much influence over the minds of America is that our heritage and traditions have been subverted so thoroughly. What's happening overseas is secondary to what's happening in our own country. You need to be thinking about first and foremost, your family and then the community around you.

20.

"If you worship your enemy, you are defeated.
If you adopt the enemy's religion, you are enslaved.
If you breed with your enemy, you are destroyed."
-Polydorus of Sparta

Blood is the basis of a strong country.

You cannot ignore van den Berghe because he's a leftist realizing that the Communist views on class distinction are secondary to race. His work is likely the foundation of the social Marxism we see today and why the founding stock American is getting dominated in his own country. The American has forgotten the importance of race. It's something built into our DNA. You cannot reject reality and expect to survive. Look at California which had a population of 94% White in 1950 and is now at 36% in 2018.

When you look at America, two trajectories offer the opportunity for victory. You either save the founding stock or create a new race. Either way requires the importance of family to be put to the forefront. Our powerful history of conquest on the American frontier is demonized. How many personal, family stories do you remember? How many were told to you? How many of your ancestors do you know about and are worth remembering? You get the "official narrative," which of course is also demonized as bad Whitey killing off poor Indians. But the personal, familial histories are mostly lost.

The Romans made busts of their ancestors and worshipped them like Gods. The Greks too had this kind of ancestor worship. It wasn't all about the Gods and heroes. They had an understanding that the dead had to be remembered and had to be taken care of. If you didn't have sons and daughters to honor you after your death, your soul would starve and die. You can also look at this from the viewpoint of man mastering space and doing what he can to keep it conquered. The ancients must have either witnessed or heard stories of people getting wiped out, bloodlines ended so they made these traditions to keep their line strong.

It was the duty of the father to make his sons warriors. To forge alliances with his kin to aid each other when circumstances became dire. One way of doing this was exchanging daughters which helped the fitness of the tribe as a whole. They had support networks. Families would produce many children which then could depend on each other when the parents passed. They also had many uncles and cousins they could call on. How many family members or friends can you call on today? These support networks have been gutted and replaced by "dem programs."

21.

Kin over Country

Country is important to me. Globohomo must pay for what it's done to our country. I want to honor the real America. I want to see the return of cowboys and frontiersmen. We need new pathfinders, but none of this can happen with the love-for-country conservatives being the bulwark of the right. It can't happen if our best men get gutted in worthless police actions overseas while our government ships in foreigners to replace Americans. Could you honestly see our ancestors — and even the founding fathers — supporting what America has become? They would be repulsed to the point of violence.

What's happening abroad doesn't matter. What matters is building a new culture and that begins first with the FAMILY. Most don't realize how circumstances can change in an instant. How easy it is for the regime to crush families. Misfortune can strike in such a manner as to leave a man believing he is the modern incarnation of the biblical Job. Something like this has happened to one of my family members and I worry about him daily. Most of us are a couple of steps from ruin and don't realize how fast and hard misfortune can strike.

You have to begin reforging the kind of networks are forefathers did. This is more important than the daily outrages of the regime. You need to become more self-reliant. Where you need help, choose kin over dem programs. Have more sons and daughters. Much of my own family is splintered, primarily by distance, but also by turmoil. Try to be close to family and when it's not possible, try to instill it into your children.

The government picked up all the slack and took all the power from the vacuum created when they destroyed the family. This course can only be reversed by taking back that power and responsibility. The most important thing is to make your family strong and resilient against the psychological warfare of the enemy. Forge alliances with like-minded men. The state has a monopoly on violence now, but back in early America, all men had to become warriors or risk being scalped in an Indian raid. We are under similar circumstances to the early settlers in this respect. You owe it to your family to become a warrior in your own right and to pass this down to your sons.

Much of the counterargument is how the state will come down hard on our people if they try to do what's right. They tried to do the state's job and so, the state will punish them for this. This is a cope argument. Strong people don't think like this. Winners don't think like this. What did Southerners do during Reconstruction after just losing a war, when great injustices were being committed against them? They formed the KKK. The KKK wasn't formed to lynch blacks, though they did that later, it was formed to deal with the crimes being committed against their own by the state carpetbaggers.

22.

A Warrior Religion will either save the American or forge the next superior race. It starts with you. You must create and maintain a vigilant and manly frontier spirit. Make yourself as self-reliant as possible. Make your support network a reliance on kin, not the state. By kin, I mean both family and race. Perhaps, we must bring back oaths beyond the ones soldiers take when they join the military. Oaths of blood between men.

Make your people oriented towards conquest. The conquest of this gay regime. If the state is going to come down hard on you for doing what's right, how can you get around this? How can you practice frontier vengeance and not get caught? This is how you must think. Don't think for a second that the perpetrators don't know what they're doing. James LaFond said the "Bantu warriors" as he calls black youths, know what they are. They know what they're for.

But the Bantu are a small problem. The real problem is the left which is primarily made up of our OWN. They too — know what they're for. They know what they're doing. Yes, they are subverted, but they know what they want: the destruction of the American race. Almost all Americans alive today aren't responsible for the so-called sins the leftists are mad about.

If our people were as dangerous and bad as leftists claim(which I wish was true), every national guard group in the country would have been deployed by now. We would be under military occupation or gathered into camps as National Guardsmen hunt down these militant neo-Nazi, KKK skinheads, and peckerwoods. But it's all wet dreams for the left. Most of us are just barely getting by. Living paycheck to paycheck, just trying not to get fired. Most are so blissfully unaware of the problem; they don't know how their son all of the sudden believes he's a girl.

You have to anticipate how globohomo is going to strike. Be strategic-minded. All this ridiculous crime happens all over the country, but the second you — Whitey — do something about it, the state comes down hard on you. How much of that is true and how much of it is you being afraid to act? You don't have to join the military to become a warrior. It helps a lot to be sure, but then you risk horrible maiming just to make sure Afghanis can sign up for dem programs at your expense while also taking the job opportunities that would have gone to your children because they are "dreamers."

23.

Do everything you can to build up yourself and your kin. They want you to be blackpilled. To be demoralized. They want the situation to appear hopeless. Always be looking for the path to victory. Be strategic and methodical. What you can't finish in your lifetime, leave to your children. That is PURPOSE. This is the great task of our blood, to reclaim the country back from our enemies. If we have to overthrow America to reclaim America, so be it.

Don't be tied down to the pieces of paper left behind by the founders. The papers themselves are worthless if they led to this. I'd argue the founders themselves would rebel against the pile of trash this country has become. It's the spirit of the frontiersmen you should keep, it's what made our people strong. What returned them to nature. This is the real spirit of the American, not the institutions in Washington.

I leave you with this: take care of your family above all else. Have sons and daughters, as many as you can. Teach them to reject globohomo indoctrination. Put kin over country and forge alliances with your blood. Make new oaths. Make yourself a warrior and always be on the lookout for the path to victory. Tall stories were prevalent in America when I was a kid, but you don't hear much about them anymore. You should have the goal of becoming the TALL STORY your descendants will tell their children in the future.

24.

"They will be men of race — not in the sense of today's belief in race, but in my sense of it as a matter of strong instincts, among them that superior eye for the things of reality that the cosmopolitans and authors today can no longer distinguish from the flash of mere intelligence; in short, men who feel themselves born and called to be masters." -Oswald Spengler

What does it mean to have race? This is a very important question and goal for every man. Our conception of race today comes down to the color of skin and where you hail from, but the ancients had a more primordial conception of race. You only get a hint of this conception of race when you read authors such as Ernst Jünger or Oswald Spengler. But if you want to feel and understand what it means to have race, you read *Beowulf*. *Beowulf* is a glorious testament to a hero who was the "last of his race."

If you haven't read *Beowulf* or you did do in the past, you should give it another read. It's not enough to read the classics only once. You must return to it from time to time, I remind you of Heraclitus saying that "you never step into the same river twice." This is true with the classics. You may know the story, but when you return to it, you're a different man and different lessons will be taught. When I first read *Beowulf*, it was a fun read, but I didn't pick up on nearly as much as I did the next time I read the epic.

When you examine *Beowulf*, you realize not everything is what it seems. It comes off first as a hero conquering monsters much in the way of a Thor or a Herakles. Underneath, however, are hidden meanings. The first thing you might notice is that while almost all the characters are Christian, the enemies' descendants of Cain, the Christianity of *Beowulf* seems crudely pasted on top of something much older. There is no mention of Christ, but the heroes do credit God throughout the epic — only not in the way you're accustomed to Christians doing. God is referred to as the warden of glory, the helper of heroes, and the God of Victory. He sounds more like an Olympian or Aesir God than the Christian God.

Once you see this, you can't unsee it. The tale of Beowulf becomes even more ancient when you realize these supposed "Christians" are living very much in a Pagan world. Grendel and his mother are giants. There is a dragon. Hrothgar is a descendant of Ing, a deity better known as Freyr. Halls are made and hearth fires are still being lit within them. Beowulf himself is extremely saddened when the dragon burns down his hearth.

What you also see present in *Beowulf* is Oswald Spengler's conception of race, which he touches on in his book *The Hour of Decision*. Race according to Spengler is more than the color of your skin and he disavows the proponents of "racial purity." He claims the ancients would accept someone into their tribe — no matter his color — if he showed he had race. Before we get into what it means to have race, let's talk about the "last of his race," Beowulf. Beowulf in his middle years conquers Grendel and his mother. He honorably served his King until the crown was passed down to him. It seemed this man was living a life of glory and fame, something the Ancient Greks would even admire.

When after fifty years of his reign, however, a dragon attacks his kingdom. Beowulf, now in his seventies, puts together a small war band for vengeance and glory. He sets out to take on the dragon himself, in single combat. When you first read *Beowulf*, this act of courage fires you up. You say "YES, that's RIGHT!" You want to see Beowulf go out in blazing glory. But there's a deep, hidden sadness behind the renown of the War King.

Beowulf begins his dangerous battle with the dragon. Quickly, he realizes he isn't the hero he was when he was younger. The two combatants, hero and dragon, fear each other. The dragon, however, gets the upper hand early, and when he does, something important happens. All of Beowulf's companions, save one, flee into the nearby woods. They abandon Beowulf to his fate. Wiglaf is the only companion to remain behind and comes to his King's aid. Together they conquer the dragon and claim his treasure for their people, the Geats, but Beowulf receives his death blow in the battle.

The ides of doom follow the death of the War King. The Geats fear they will soon be conquered by their rivals, the Swedes. The might of the War King was the only thing that kept their enemies at bay. He was the last of his race, though clearly, the Geats were still numerous. What is meant by race is something different. Having race according to Oswald Spengler meant having a strong will, healthy instincts, and a will to possession and power. What was left in the wake of Beowulf's death were men who lacked race. Only cowards who wouldn't fight for their people and their King.

Of all Beowulf's men, only eleven came with him to fight the dragon. Only one of them fought at his War King's side. The rest were cowards. They lacked RACE. Beowulf was a great man, but was he a "good king?" He left no men of power, men of RACE, to take his place when he died, to ensure the continued survival of the tribe. What you're experiencing when you read Beowulf is the end of a people. Not just of the Geats, but also of the Danes earlier in the epic.

The Danes couldn't even find a man of their own race to put against Grendel. They were blessed by the arrival of Beowulf. King Hrothgar of the Danes — a man of race — became too old to protect his people and failed to develop men of race to take his place. This is a glaring problem we also face today. To have race is to have a strong will and healthy instincts. To be a man of power who can protect his people. It is to be what Spengler calls the "eternal warlike and barbaric man."

Sorry end-of-history enjoyers, but history never ends(say this in your best Jonathan Bowden impression). There will be more challenges and more wars. The fight for survival will continue into eternity. You either form a race willing to meet this challenge or nature sews the seeds of your destruction as she did with the Geats and the Danes. If you truly want to see a Warrior Religion rise from this chaos, you must look to forging men of race. Men who will answer the call to battle and show heroism and excellence over all others. Without this, you're just adding to the noise.

A race needs warriors. Beowulf was a great example of a man who showed race, but as a King, he failed in inspiring and mentoring others to take on that role after he was gone. His kingdom falls soon after his death. The warrior is the primordial archetype of man. You're made to fight. You also need women of race and the quality that makes women have race — according to Spengler — is the desire to be a mother. To have children. To replenish the lives lost in wars.

25.

"Barbarism is that which I call strong race, the eternal warlike in the type of the beast-of-prey man. It often seems to have ceased to exist, but it is crouching in the soul ready to spring. Given a big challenge — and it is on top of the enemy." -Oswald Spengler

The harsh conditions of our ancestors in the New World forced them to become hard and strong. They had to fight to survive and possess the courage to make tough decisions. You saw much RACE in colonial America. America became a world power because our people became warlike and barbaric. The life sold to us by liberal democracy is a fantasy. That is not how you survive in nature. You must become a man of race. Someone with a strong will to power, someone willing to fight. To show fire and fanaticism. Nature favors the strong. Nature will always favor the strong.

A people who have race possess powerful, warlike men and women, who desire above all else, to be mothers. Both are necessary for a people to thrive. Tragedy will strike. It's inevitable. The strength of a people falls with the men's ability to raise more men of race, for women to fill the ranks of the fallen. They need also, a man of power who can govern them well and won't lead them into destruction. This — a Warrior Religion must manifest if it's to find a place in this world.

26.

Self-Exile into the Desert

In some of my earliest writing on Warrior Religions, I urged the importance of strength and survival, as well as the notion that we should self-exile as a people, at least metaphorically, to the desert. To acquire the power necessary to make change may be beyond our current reach. Reaching for this power while your foundation is a mound of quicksand is a recipe for failure. The foundation must be strong. There is a risk, however. If you abandon the hostile institutions and government, the persecution against our people can and will intensify. Oswald Spengler believed you couldn't do this; you needed the mastery of technics and politics to give your people a chance.

One may compare the situation of the Germans that Spengler was speaking to, to that of the Americans today. Was it worse or better? To that end, I believe there must be a balancing act. No, you cannot completely surrender your country to your enemies so you can go on a vision quest in the desert. However, you must put space between you and your enemies, to give your people the opportunity to build the strong foundation it requires. Those that are capable must get themselves into whatever position of power they can. Those without foundations must strive to leave one behind for their children. Make them understand that they owe a duty to their bloodline.

In this way, it helps to imagine ourselves in the position of the Romans when Hannibal crossed the Alps with fifty thousand men and war elephants. The first encounters with Hannibal were met with utter devastation. Hannibal knew how to defeat the Romans. He was a strategic genius. His one flaw you could say, was that he played by the old way of warfare, in that he expected the Romans to sue for peace after a big enough defeat. He had no desire, you can say, of sacking Rome. The Romans on the other hand, had already experienced "Vae Victus" or Woe to Conquered as it translates to, when Rome was sacked by Brennus and his Senones tribe long before Hannibal.

The Romans learned a very important lesson. One that the United States, at its core, still knows. What is this lesson? Do not lose wars. The Romans were treated very unfairly at the hands of Brennus. It's where that phrase, "Vae Victus," was first uttered. From that moment, the Romans would never admit defeat in war. No matter how badly they were defeated, they would keep fighting. Even after Hannibal killed fifty thousand Romans at Cannae, they refused to ransom with the Carthaginians, which blew the mind of Hannibal. He did not know what to do except continue with his strategy. Why do you think the United States demands unconditional surrender from its enemies?

But rewind to before the disaster at Cannae, when Roman allies were abandoning Rome to join Hannibal, how did the Romans respond? They elected a dictator named Quintus Fabius Maximus Verrucosus, better known as just Fabius. This man is incredibly underrated and not talked about enough by historians today, many of whom are too caught up with the allure of Hannibal, the barbarian who made it to the gates of Rome. Fabius is influential in AMERICAN history as many compare the campaigns of George Washington in the War for Independence to Fabius and his strategy against Hannibal which is known to antiquity as the "Fabian Strategy." Fabius is seen as the originator of what we call guerrilla warfare today. Perhaps, he was actually the God of guerrilla fighters? He wasn't so popular with the Romans during his reign as dictator however, his nickname was "The Delayer."

War historians were more friendly to him than his contemporary Romans, who did not understand Hannibal as well as Fabius. Fabius saw Hannibal for who he was: a man of power and a great tactical genius. He did the only thing he could for the Romans: buy them time and build their confidence. One should note that the Battle of Cannae, the famous victory of Hannibal, did not happen under the reign of Fabius, but directly after, as overzealous consuls walked into a trap. Fabius made no tactical errors against Hannibal and maintained that his one goal was the salvation of Rome, no matter the accusations of betrayal or cowardice that made against his character. His first act as dictator was to reinsure the Romans that they were not inferior to Hannibal, a sentiment that was growing among the reeling Romans. Rather, the Romans had neglected proper worship of The Gods and Hannibal was punishment for this.

Fabius demanded great sacrifices be made to The Gods to make up for their neglect of worship. He was also a strong believer in the numerological significance of the number 3, demanding that each citizen spend 333 sestertii and 333 denarii at the festivals. Wat means? In his war against Hannibal, he earned his nickname because he refused to engage the Carthaginians. He made sure to always put his legions on the high ground and trailed the barbarian army. Fabius ordered guerrilla campaigns against Hannibal in the form of a scorched earth policy that burned food supplies and harassing Carthaginian scavengers, never letting Hannibal rest. He took up posts that Hannibal would not attack and never took any bait left for him by the Carthaginian. He refused to fall for traps.

This type of war is not sexy. It did not have the victories you saw with Caesar later on, rather Fabius was buying Rome time to regroup. They had lost a few legions to Hannibal and Fabius understood that their course of action was not sustainable in the long run. He knew that Hannibal was far from home and his enemy's resources were finite. The longer he could keep Hannibal in Italy, the more likely the scales would tip in the favor of Rome. It allowed the Romans to foundation build. To forge new legions and tactics. It made them believe they could win and made them want the fight(even when they weren't yet ready for it).

Many on our side want a Caesar. A walking God-man who throws thunderbolts at our enemies. Caesar gets a lot of credit, much of which is well deserved. However, the legions he had were professional armies put together in the reforms under Gaius Marius. This is something Fabius did not have. Many on our side want a Caesar, but what we need is a Fabius. A man that can rescue our people from its current calamity. Who can stop the bleeding and build the foundation for a harder people from which a Caesar can rise.

Look at our current leaders. Who among them looks like a Caesar? Who among them looks like they even have a chance of challenging our enemies for territory? There is no one. Trump was the last to challenge their sovereignty, but he would not cross the Rubicon. He would not do what it would take to win. Our foundation is SAND, hell, it might even be quicksand. You will not win from such a position.

A stronger foundation must be built. Space must be made between us and our enemies to allow room for the growth of harder men. This is the path. Look for a Fabius, not a Caesar. If you must exile yourself to the desert to accomplish this, so be it. If you are capable, you should seek out power. If you are not capable, then you must strive to be so. Whatever the case, you must fly under the radar of our enemies. Grow in the shadows so that you can strike like the thunderbolt when the time arises.

27.

You don't understand the importance of fire. It's sacred to man and perhaps, the material of creation itself. The Ancient Grek philosopher, Heraclitus, believed the universe was "ever-living fire, kindling itself by regular measures and going out by regular measures."

28.

The Sacred Fire

The Ancient Greeks and Romans both had similar Pagan pantheons. These pantheons, however, weren't as important as we give them credit for. In Greece for example, there were still mystery cults centered around the prior pantheon called the Titans. Further, both peoples had domestic religions and Gods. Yes, each family had their own religion and Gods. You've heard about decentralized bitcoin, what do you think about decentralized religions? This is very interesting, compare to our modern era where culture is very much homogeneous in comparison. There were similarities between the families: each family had a Sacred Fire they kept lit at all times.

The sacred hearth was of extreme importance to the ancients. It's said that when Agamemnon returned home from the Trojan War, the first thing he did was not pay tribute to Zeus or any of the Olympians but visit his family's sacred hearth. This custom completely changes how we should view the Greeks and Romans. These rites and customs are primordial even to the Greek and Roman religions. Modern society has separated us from what our ancestors viewed as important for survival. The first separation is man and War. From the earliest beginnings, man had to fight, he had to go to war, in order to survive. Do you not think nature selected for strong, warlike men?

Look back to the development of mankind and you will find a different hierarchy of values to what we worship today. The preachers of progressivism might ask why does it matter? We've "progressed." It matters because we've fundamentally moved away from what's natural to man, what makes us strong, what fills us with power and purpose. We're in the process of being milked like cows for everything we're worth. A people with no understanding of who they are or where they come from are easy to control and easy to manipulate.

It doesn't take much to imagine how man formed his hierarchy of values. The first men were engaged in the true struggle: the fight for survival. From the fight for survival came the ancestor cults, individual families honoring the forefathers who got their bloodline through the hard times.

They fought different now-extinct humanoids, competing tribes, sabertooth tigers, and hunted mammoths. In addition, they had to battle nature and all that entails. Extreme heat or cold and everything in between. Blizzards, volcanos, hurricanes, earthquakes, and thunderstorms. Fighting, surviving, and strength were the first values.

Sometime after the development of stone and wood tech, likely for weapons, came the discovery of fire. The discovery of fire must have been a tale for the ages. It's said with certainty that fire was around at least 300,000 years ago found alongside stone tools and hand axes, but there is evidence of it possibly being around as far back as 1.5 million years ago meaning it could have been Homo Erectus that first controlled the flame. Fire is very primordial to man, and it was the tool in which man conquered the world. Through fire, many changes took place in man. The cooking of food helped make the brain larger. The campfire forged culture, language, and religion.

29.

Fire is one of the oldest Gods.

You have to wonder how man came to discover fire. How was the tale passed down through the ages? Most of us are familiar with the Greek telling of fire. The Titan Prometheus stole fire from Zeus and gave it to man. Prometheus was eternally punished for this transgression against The Gods. Zeus bound him to a rock and had an eagle come every day to eat out his liver. The liver would grow back overnight so Prometheus could be punished every day for eternity. It's interesting to note that the Ancient Greks believed emotions came from the liver, so you see why Zeus had an eagle eat out his liver. The most excruciating punishment for the most terrible sacrilege.

Fire for primitive man made him sovereign over his domain. It became a man's world after the discovery of fire. Fire helped man to think. It gave him warmth and protection from the elements. It allowed him to speak with the other men of his tribe. Fire became a destructive force to be unleashed on man's enemies. Fire was energy to be unleashed and he who had the most energy was usually victorious in war.

By the time of the Ancient Greks — and who knows how long before them — the sacred hearth was present in the homes of men. Fire became their God. They worshipped the fire as much as they worshipped their ancestors. Both of which held more importance than the Olympians and Titans that get taught to the normies. When a man married, he had to carry his wife before the sacred hearth and perform the necessary rites to induct her into their domestic religion. We can only hope to imagine how rich a culture these so-called primitives had.

Each family had its own religion, customs, and traditions. These were likely forged in that family's fight for survival. They must have had a keen understanding of what it took for their ancestors to survive and get to the point where they had land and a home. They must have felt fire played a huge part in getting them to that point and did everything in their power to keep that fire going. Can you imagine how many rites and traditions are simply lost to us? It may seem foreign to the modern looking back at them, but if you could see where they came from, it will all make sense.

30.
The Sacred Fire is also within you.

The Sacred Fire was more than a tool and weapon to the first men. It left its mark on them. It was a symbol of the Sacred Fire within them. In each man is a fire. A will to power. A will to master space. The fire in men's souls is primordial. When you live in accordance with nature, your fire grows. When you devote yourself to leftist progressive hellscape, your fire is smothered out.

Think of your will as fire. How do you increase the inner flame? How do you prevent it from burning out? Furthermore, how can you combine that fire with the fire of your people and ignite a firestorm? A purifying conflagration. These are the things the first men had to think about. How can he steel his heart for the struggles, the battles, and the wars ahead of him?

The Sacred Fire inspired man. It offered protection, warmth, and a chance for reflection. Maybe for the ancients, the Sacred Fire ignited their own inner fire. You must imagine the inner fire within yourself. What makes that fire grow? What starves it? Take note of each and build your life around forging a powerful inner flame.

Fire and fanaticism are worth more to you and our side than the deepest intellectualism. Theology is as important only so far as it fans the flames of our passion. The foundations of a Warrior Religion require fire and fanaticism over everything else. It's not enough to say you believe in God. A tranny can say they "believe" in God. How much are you willing to sacrifice for that belief? How hard are you willing to fight for it?

That's what matters. Not what you believe, but the fire and fanaticism that burns inside you. The culture should be shaped around creating the mightiest of purifying fires. A fire that will cleanse away the blight of your enemies. What is it that creates this fire and fanaticism in you? How can you make that fire grow? Find the people who are also devoted to your cause.

The world isn't kind to the reactionary. You have to be proactive in what you want to bring into the world. Take steps, no matter how small, to make that world possible. Do not live in the intellectualist frame. Be a forger of worlds and peoples.

Don't make excuses, look for opportunities, look for solutions. Keep moving forward.

31.

The fight for survival is a matter of all men. It's also the great unifier of men. It's easy to forget this in the age of comfort and decadence we live in today. But you must remember. You must get closer to the darkness, to the primitive, to be gifted this wisdom. Like Woden hanging from the world tree, stuck with a spear, to learn the secret of the runes. The brotherhood of armed men was the origin of the first tribes, orders, and peoples. From this brotherhood came kingdoms, nations, and empires.

These men came together to survive and continue their bloodlines. Something the modern never thinks about is his blood and where it comes from. If you're alive today, if you're reading this, you're part of a bloodline that extends back to the very beginning of mankind. Your blood is the blood of the first men. What did your ancestors have to go through to make you possible? How many world-ending events? How many wars and plagues? How far did they have to venture out into the unknown, into the frontier?

The enemy wants you to believe that blood, that race, isn't important. Science says we're all mostly the same. They want you to forsake the primordial brotherhood established by the first men. But not even the leftist can deny the power of your bloodline. They have no answer to this. It ain't about believing so much that you are superior, but about understanding that your blood goes back to the beginning, and you have ancestors who went through hell to keep the fire going. You're just the latest representative of that Sacred Fire, of that blood, and you owe a duty to your ancestors who came before you.

When you see the world through the eyes of your ancestors, you can truly understand how terrible a crime it is for the leftist to become the ignoble end of his bloodline whether through choosing not to have children or mutilating himself in such a way as he can't. The worst crime is to mindfuck your people into these attitudes that allow the Sacred Fires to go out. To hide from them their ancestral heritage and the responsibilities of that heritage. The duty to your bloodline. This is the great evil in the world today. The evil that must be destroyed at all costs. But you must first remember what's in the blood and take control of your bloodline.

Who are you to be ashamed of your blood? What kind of arrogance(or bigotry?) must a man have to want to kill his bloodline? Not out of the sense of duty to his family and comrades or the seeking out of a glorious death, but of shame and guilt over the alleged actions of some of his ancestors told to him by the very same people that hate him because of his race. Ashamed of a perceived history he has no hope of ever verifying because as we know, history is written by the victors. How much of it was wrong or simply made up? The crimes we suffer through today are the most grievous of crimes. You owe your life to the many who came before you and it's your duty to keep the Sacred Fire going. It's the most terrible of crimes to consciously go against this.

32.

The patriarchy is the point of ire to the deranged lunatics of the left. Something they want destroyed. For the ancients, the PATER was the priest and representative of his family's Gods, charged with the protection of the family and the hearth for a period of time that ended with his death. This ancient, domestic religion is where we see the values of duty and dignity emerge in mankind. It can be hard to relate to the rites of these men because when we gain knowledge of these domestic religions, they were already far into development. The Pater was in charge of an already established household and land.

It was understood that the Sacred Fire and the family tomb were of immense importance. When an ancestor died, he became a God of the domestic religion, and it was up to his descendants to take care of the rites and traditions of the bloodline. Also understand that when the ancients sat down to eat a meal, they left a plate for their ancestors. They believed the spirits of their dead ancestors still walked the grounds of their land, protecting them — but they had to be fed or they would turn hungry and haunt the family. This is the origin of ghost stories. For the most part, we understand death differently, but you can see how they depended on the rites of the family to preserve the family. In Rome, the way they made sure a man couldn't be remembered and worshipped was to invade his family's tomb and steal his body so his descendants couldn't worship him.

The domestic religions eventually got too much into the religion aspect and lost the purpose from which they were established. One example Coulanges' *The Ancient City* gives is a Pater who dies without a male heir. The religion demanded his estate go to the closest male relative who was then made to marry the deceased Pater's daughter. The closest male relative would have to hand over his entire estate to a son, including his wife, so he could take charge of his relative's estate. The daughter, if she was married, would be forced to get a divorce so she could marry this male relative. At a certain point, the domestic religion became unnatural, religion for the sake of religion. You must look instead to its original purpose.

The domestic religions cared about male bloodlines. Why? It was the men who went to war to defend family and tribe. It was men who could bring glory to the bloodline. This hasn't changed much. A woman can do these things now, but it's not as prevalent. War is still primarily fought and won by men.

The Sacred Fire is your bloodline. Your bloodline doesn't just belong to you. It belongs also to your ancestors who did their duty for the blood. Now it's your turn. You must do what it takes to survive, to have sons, and instill in them the same duty to the blood. The hearth fire of the ancients represented this duty all men are bound to. There's scientific reasoning for this, but it's not important to know. What's important is your devotion to this Sacred Fire.

33.

Values such as pride, honor, glory, dignity, and duty come from the domestic religion and the ancestor cults.

There is a deep blood memory connected to the hearth fire. One that we don't appreciate today, but the ancients must have. Imagine what it must have been like for the son of the man who discovered fire. His father must have lived on in the fire he taught him to create. The warmth of the fire was the protection of his father. Later on, down the road when his descendants claimed land for their blood, the father, his sons, and their sons made oaths to keep the Sacred Fire lit. To never let the fire go out.

In the fire, the Pater saw his own father who had shown him how to make fire and survive in nature. He will go on to teach his children how to make fire, like the ancestors who came before him. A rite of passage, perhaps? The essential skill of man, the skill that gave man an unfair advantage over the other beasts of prey. Do you see now how the ancients came to see the hearth fire as a God? Why even a king of kings like Agamemnon would first go to his hearth fire after finally returning home from Troy? It is the primordial relationship, the Thread of Continuity, that we have had severed in modern times. The bond between father, son, and the ancestors. The Sacred Fire, the Sacred Bloodline.

You must remember this in dark times. Remember that your blood is special. It goes back to the beginning of man. How many bloodlines have been snuffed out of existence? Yet yours remains. The opportunity for glory and fame remains. For greatness.

But do not forget the duty owed to your bloodline, to the Sacred Fire. The honor and dignity owed to your family. The fight to survive is an eternal struggle, to keep one's blood worthy of God. The moment the bloodline stops being worthy of God, God — through nature — will sow the seeds of its destruction. It's not about just you. You have a duty to not just your family and tribe, but to the blood and the Sacred Fire and those who will come after you.

34.
Mankind's Biological Imperative

This modern world of ours is a godless world. Our children are raised by the state for at least twelve years to unlearn what we already know in the blood. We are given a "scientific" reason for how mankind came about. They learn "powerful" ideas like there is no reason for our existence. There is no difference between races except for skin color. Why then, would we have different skin colors, if not for a reason? Our people do not dare to ask that question.

Even the most average of men can come to terms with the reality that he has a biological imperative. Mankind as a whole has a biological imperative. You go to school for so long in order to unlearn your biological instincts. To teach you how to ignore what your body is telling you to do. This allows evil men to manipulate you toward their own ends. Your indoctrination, however, is rarely made complete. You cannot erase thousands upon thousands of years of blood memories passed down from father to son, mother to daughter.

The most potent of mankind's biological imperatives is the need to procreate. Every young man and woman experiences this. It overrides every other desire. It's true in our time, that people do not always answer the call, but they suffer for this decision their entire lives. Mankind's most important biological imperative is to survive. Since a man cannot live forever, he renews his blood through the children he leaves behind. They are then charged with keeping the Sacred Fire lit and performing their duty to the blood.

The vilest souls are the ones who choose to be the ignoble end of their bloodlines. Perhaps, it's not entirely their fault. The indoctrination into modern society is a persuasive force to those who don't have a strong family to guide them through the storm. To allow them to influence our people, however, is a great crime against our race.

35.

If you examine the scientific theories for life, you see why there is a biological imperative in the first place. Many believe in the idea of a "Big Bang." Those of the Christian faith believe man was created in the image of God and so they will quickly discount the ideas of their theological enemies. I will ask you, however, to consider how life sprang from the Big Bang. There is a common saying that once you delve into science, you become an atheist, but the deeper you dig, you find God again. There is "intelligent design" to our universe.

It is said that the human body is made up of around one hundred trillion cells. Of these cells, there are around two hundred different types. You cannot see the cell without the power of a telescope. They are smaller than the human eye can distinguish. To take the scientific idea of how life came about, you start with just a single cell. Our body is of one mind but made up of trillions of cells, all united in the fight for survival. All these cells are devoted to giving the greater organism power. It would not surprise me if one day mankind learned that the earth itself was just a CELL of much more titanic organism.

In order for cells to survive, they divide. The time means little to me, but for millions or billions of years, life existed as single-cell organisms. Whenever a cell found itself wrong, or malformed, it would quarantine itself from the rest. It had its own self-destruct mechanism to protect the whole. As they ate through resources, they would have to take to the frontier to find new space to master. Watching the activity of a cell is a path to understanding the doctrines of nature.

What you see on the cellular level can be observed in mankind today. When a tribe used up its resources, it would have to move to a new area. People who get struck with things such as depression often times quarantine themselves from the rest of the tribe.

36.

Whether we were made in the image of God or evolved from a single-cell organism, we practice natural law. We know natural law by instinct, it takes over a dozen years of public education to indoctrinate it out of you. Much about getting your life in order is letting go of the trauma caused by your liberal education. It's not that all of education is bad, rather it is the blind leading the blind. Truth has surrendered itself to feelings. You cannot have true science when the politically incorrect science gets buried by cowards. The influence of very bad people has left its mark on the pursuit of truth.

I believe we were created in the image of God. Our domination of the planet has convinced me that not only are we made in the image of God, but we are also chosen by God. We have a greater purpose that's beyond our current understanding. To gain knowledge of this understanding, you have to understand mankind's biological imperative. Certainly, the extent to which the blood acts upon us is unknown and if it is known, it is buried, hidden from our eyes. You must begin by rejecting the liberal idea that the only difference between races is skin color. Even if we are about 2% different biologically, how many differences are they hiding in that 2%? What is 2% of a hundred trillion? How is that not significant?

There is no way of knowing how mankind began. The prevailing science says that man came out of Africa. What's to say he didn't come out of many different places? The differences in race come down to where our people came out of and the requirements for survival there. The soil changes the man. Not all men are created equal. There is a natural hierarchy, a pecking order, in all things.

Differences in race go beyond skin color. Pierre van den Berghe found that race is perceived as an extension of kin. A man would rather have a tyrant of his own race than a tyrant of another race. Racial distinction trumps all other distinctions. The idea of Communism never took off because it was crushed by ethnic politics. Every time you try to manipulate mankind away from racial identification, it always came back with a vengeance.

Now one may argue that communism is still around today. That the enemies of God are pursuing this ideology. In some ways, its proponents will say they believe in these ideas, but the main driver of their movements is always ethnic hatred. You see this manifest today with the anti-White vitriol launched at Americans. The ideology is secondary to the ethnic strife. In other ways, the ideology of today is made into a new theology. It is built upon the foundation established by Christianity which it wears as a skin suit.

The holocaust and slavery have taken the place of Jesus Christ. Blacks the new chosen people, persecuted by the evil White Man. But it is all ethnic strife goaded on by elites, who want more power and money. Now you may want to move past race. To be "color blind," but this is folly. You cannot change the minds of every man, woman, and child. It takes but one bad actor to crush this kind of thinking. Rather, I ask you to remember the discussion above on cells.

Individualism is big in modern society. You think of yourself as an individual even though you're made up of a hundred trillion cells. The power of mankind is not in the individual, it's in the race. You are an individual, but you belong to a race. There have been no multi-ethnic empires. Now the empires may employ different races, but these races were segregated from each other. They all had their own lands and their own armies.

You gain power by the racial cohesion of your people and lose power by the same principle. Men of the same race are capable of trusting each other on a greater level than men of different races. God has built this into mankind. Different races can be allies or enemies. Our "liberal democracy" likes to talk about the importance of diversity. "Diversity is our strength." But you cannot preserve diversity without segregation.

You cannot control the destiny of other races; you can only control your own. Some may shoot for the stars; others be content with a mud hut in Africa. God has preordained the fate and course of all. As a species, we operate best while segregated by race. A race can work together to reach the stars. A multi-ethnic empire will descend into unquenchable ethnic strife.

What you see happening today isn't the triumph of diversity. It's the melting down of all culture into nothing. We're being made into worker ants and consumers to be milked for all we're worth. Diversity is our strength. It may be necessary for the survival of the species, but what we have today is not diversity. It's the melting down of all values and distinctions with the destruction of the White race at the forefront.

37.

You have blood memories passed down from your ancestors. You must remember them. The world will reveal itself to you when you do.

A species doesn't make it long without the capability to learn and adapt. To pass down the lessons learned to the next generation. A Thread of Continuity. The scientific understanding of the human body is far from complete. I believe in true science, but nothing trumps the blood memories and instincts of your body.

38.

A biological imperative less talked about is man's need to master space. Resources are limited. If you want to grow, you will have to seek out new space or be forced to cull your ranks. When presented with new space to master and conquer, a people flourish. The last time we saw this in history is the American conquest of the New World. Our people expanded from sea to shining sea within a hundred years. Birthrates were off the charts despite having none of the comforts and technology we enjoy today.

What is mastering space? Friedrich Nietzsche believed man had an inherent Will to Power. I believe man has an inherent will to master the space and conditions he's born into. The two ideas are not opposed, rather they complement each other. You want power in order to master space. Men have a biological calling to do this. When they do master space, their blood calls upon them to look beyond their borders. To go further into the unknown.

This drive to master space pushes mankind out into the furthest frontiers. He who takes to the frontier and conquers becomes changed next to the people he left behind. This creates real diversity and increases the chances of mankind's continued survival. You may start with just wanting to master the space around you, but the blood will call you to the furthest frontier to renew the race.

In Nazi Germany, there was a similar idea called lebensraum. Lebensraum meant living space or rather the living space required for a people's natural development. The Germans believed they didn't have enough living space and had the idea of expanding into their frontier — at the expense of peoples living in the Balkans and Russia — to increase their living space. Now the theory behind this idea is not wrong, but it's also not complete. The Germans weren't allowed to accomplish this mission thanks to the intervention of the United States and England. The reality is there is no natural living space. Any space they acquired by conquest would end up not being enough over a long enough timeline. This isn't some attack against the "insatiable" desires of the Nazis, it is true for all peoples.

39.

The Americans took over the United States in similar fashion. Sea to shining sea. Was that enough? Was it enough to acquire the Louisiana Purchase? No, Americans went after Texas. And then, California. Going to war with Mexico to make it happen. They saw territories above like Oregon and Washington and knew they had to get those too.

The phrase used to describe the feeling and sentiments of Americans was MANIFEST DESTINY. Americans were chosen by God to tame the wilderness of the New World. They overcame native Indians, Mexicans, Frenchmen, and Englishmen to do it. Nothing would stop them from possessing the United States. Maybe the sight of the Pacific stilled the American desire for more land. Maybe it was the disappointment that there wasn't any more land to take. The frontiers seemingly vanished next to the mighty ocean before them. Why did Americans stop at the Pacific Ocean?

Now we've picked up a little more land since then, such as Hawaii and Alaska, but the winds of conquest seemingly died out. It could be that going beyond the United States would put Americans in vulnerable positions that are not just easily defended. Maybe Americans were already spread thin across the country. Maybe they had carved out the required living space to prosper. It could be that we saw that there was no more frontier, no more unknown land. The world had become, using the words of Bronze Age Pervert, owned space.

40.

The reasons why we have stopped looking for the frontier are important. The hesitations must be overcome. Mankind's biological imperative is to survive and to survive you have to do what man's done since the beginning: dominate on the world stage. No other species has accomplished what we have. Through science, we have discovered that there is more beyond the earth, and through science, we have seen a myriad of ways of how the earth will end. This puts mankind in a precarious position. We are a species with all its eggs in one basket.

If mankind can't move beyond the earth, the story is over. Whether it be the death of our sun or some random strike from a meteor, mankind is vulnerable while we remain on Earth. From our very beginnings, we've been driven to the frontier. To do things we never thought of or thought impossible. To grow beyond our fathers. To do what they never dreamed of doing. It's my belief that we shall not know God again until this is done. Until we get back to the frontier.

41.

The fight for survival is a matter of all men.

Relative comfort and advances in technology have made our people forget this biological imperative. It's easy to believe nature doesn't matter anymore. That we've moved beyond nature. But we've never left the arena. Forgetting the virtues necessary to survive in nature is a fatal flaw pushing our people toward the edge. Each war since the beginning of mankind has only gotten more massive and cataclysmic. The death tolls of the first two World Wars are beyond the mind's comprehension.

Each war has continued the minimize the role of the warrior in war. If the Ancient Grek hoplite's chances of survival and victory depended on 80% his martial excellence and 20% fortune, the modern soldier's odds are completely inverted. It's your duty to increase that percentage, to take control of your fate as much as a man can. You are a steward of your bloodline while you live, and you must make preparations for the future of your race and bloodline. Our people face a precarious position. On the one hand, our country appears to be on the top of the food chain, but we have become the pay pigs of a hostile anti-White empire. Our people are exploited at home and our best warriors are sent overseas to have their legs blown off in police actions that don't support the sovereignty of our people. On top of this, our leaders in their arrogance believe they can fend off the other two major world powers at the same time.

The fight for survival affects us all. Life upon the earth is warfare as said in the Bible. Our grandparents and great-grandparents were defeated by victory. Coming out on top of the World Wars, they were allowed to forget their survival instincts and made to be nice and plump, to be milked by gangster capital. Our children are raised into the world to be exploited. They aren't taught race instincts or the virtues of survival.

Many want to believe they just have to start the rebellion for our people to show their superiority again. To reestablish dominance over our country. This is a naïve train of thought.

The damage done to our people won't be corrected overnight. Foundation building is the most important first step for reclaiming power. Reforging the bonds between our kin. Making our people clannish and ferocious again.

The road ahead is long and unforgiving. You must become a warrior. You must forge brotherhoods with other warriors. There are no short-term solutions, only long-term planning. You have to look beyond your life. How can you prepare your sons to carry on the fight? Furthermore, how can you do these things while remaining under the radar of the elite?

Our people are raised under a fantasy worldview. A worldview that doesn't hold up in the doctrines of nature. A worldview that would crumble the moment our elite take a step too far. What would happen when the colossus comes crashing down? Will our people be crushed under its enormous weight? This is what you have to begin to think about. How do you survive? How can you take power if it does fall or wrestle power from the elite before it does fall?

The great men in history cannot be accounted for. They come into the great game like a force of nature. The proven means of survival of a people is racial cohesion. This isn't something you can do alone. You have to forge alliances with your blood. Unite under a common purpose and prepare your young to take the reins when your time is done. This is the most pressing matter: the formation of war bands and brotherhoods.

Ignore the fight for survival at your own peril.

42.

Men and women are both necessary for the survival of mankind. One should understand that woman holds a higher value. Without women producing offspring, your people die out. A woman's ability to reproduce is sacred to a people and must be honored as much as the ideal of a man as warrior.

Men are the R&D arm of mankind. They're meant to go out and test their ideas against nature. The bad ideas die out, the good ideas live on. Some manage to get their bloodline to the next generation; few leave their marks on the world. Man is a dart thrown by God at a dart board. Some stick, and some miss the mark. Ultimately, he is expendable compared to woman.

43.

Life is about preparing yourself for death. Did you do your duty to the blood? The best among us achieve undying fame. They turn the wheel of mankind.

What will you do with your life?

PART TWO:
FINDING GOD THROUGH NATURE

44.

Paganism in the Modern Day

I've been unkind to Christians. I respect that my ancestors were Christian, but they were Pagan as well. I support any Christian sect that shows it will fight and win against the enemy, but I believe leftism itself, is made primarily to combat the world religion, Christianity. Pagans have felt the world-feeling of their ancestors, with the help of philosophers like Nietzsche or authors like Robert E Howard. They understand what natural law requires, but the RELIGIOUS FEELING of their Pagan ancestors has been snuffed out of history. Forgotten to time.

There are two types of Pagans you encounter online. The first is the one who has read Nietzsche and understands the spirit of Paganism. The other is of the longhouse type that demands some return to one of the old Pantheons and if you're not following the little of what we know about them, you're just a pretender who's never read a book or lifted a weight. The latter will never amount to anything because they are LEFTIST in spirit, demanding their religion be studied and deconstructed, practiced in the same way as our ancestors without knowing what way that was. You cannot return to the old faith. You can only go forward. If you can't capture the hearts and minds of the people you need on your side to win, you'll amount to nothing.

The longhouse Pagans are as bad as the Christians who tell you the only way to get out of this mess is to go to church and pray to Jesus. They have no solutions, no ideas, they're just mad that you aren't a Pagan purist(of whatever denomination they are). No matter how hard they scream and whine online, they will never recover that lost religious feeling. They will never believe in The Gods the way their ancestors believed in The Gods. It's not wrong of them to HONOR their ways, I do. The Ancient Greks and Romans represent the point of origin for Western peoples. Every country since Rome has wanted to become Rome.

But if you want to talk about religion and religious feeling, you had better step up your game. Religion is best described by Oswald Spengler as another word for existence. It encompasses more than just a Pantheon, it's a blueprint for living life. How you live today is part of your religion. All the old religions were conquered by Christianity. Christianity has been conquered by the new religion leftism. The world is moving in the direction of the people that hate us, imagine what happens when this religion merges itself with something like Christianity. You can argue theology is leftism's only missing component.

You have to step up your game if you want to compete with this. Show your religion to be superior. It has to dominate the enemy in the field. The way to do this is to get your disciples reacquainted with NATURAL LAW. The law of tooth and claw. Those who follow the doctrines of nature find themselves favored by God himself. No matter how comfortable and decadent this society has become, we're still a part of nature. The moment hubris gets you and you forget this truth is the moment nature sows the seeds of your destruction.

With that in mind, I want to talk about what I see as NECESSARY qualities of a new Paganism to rise in our modern day. One normie interpretation of Christianity or monotheism vs Paganism is the worship of one God vs many. It's worth noting that the Romans considered monotheism to be atheism. How could you expect one God to rule over everything? C'mon man. That said, almost all of mankind now believes there is either one God or none. The Romans, however, saw the value of taking in foreign Gods to cement alliances and loyalty in their empire. The problem is that tolerance ultimately led to Christianity and their downfall.

The best way to approach this subject is, to be honest. We don't know the divine anymore. It would be wise to assume, as the Romans did, that there are many Gods and demons in the world. It would fit with our spiritual origins. In the early days of the Greks and Romans, each family had its own religion and its own Gods. Not only that, but ancestor worship, which is rarely talked about today was of vital importance to our ancestors. Through comparative mythology, we know almost all Aryan peoples had a Sky Father God who acted as King of the Pantheons and creator of mankind.

45.

As our people have strayed far from the Golden Path, it's important to acknowledge God and understand that while we don't know the nature of God, we know what he selects for in nature as evidenced by human history. The people — Christian or Pagan — that adhered to the doctrines of nature found themselves loved by God. One consideration I've had is if God selects for the races that best master the doctrines of nature and this mastery requires a people to be WARLIKE, that the Sky Father and War God may indeed be a singular role. If the most brutal and savage races seem to rise to the top, then our God must be a War God. Of course, being warlike is just part of the equation with other qualities such as wisdom, cunning, and excellence. I like the image of SCYTHIAN ARES demanding the right arms of our enemies as sacrifice and proof of our devotion to Him. Every God demands blood as sacrifice, the Christian God is no different.

We don't know the nature of God or what he wants. We know he favors the people who prove themselves superior in nature. It's best to listen to Heraclitus in this matter: we are children in comparison to The Gods and can't hope to understand the way of God. Maybe he's a child playing a board game. He may be the creator of man, but that doesn't make him loyal to man as seen by the fall of civilizations and empires. If you stray too far from His Golden Path or anger him, you can expect all the fire and brimstone of the Old Testament. Whatever the nature of God, you must have him on your side. You must be loved by God.

46.

The next important factor in the resurgence of Paganism is the proper worship of FIRE. Heraclitus believed the world was made by fire. Fire is sacred and primordial to mankind. The discovery of fire gave mankind an unfair advantage over all of nature. We've yet to be removed from the top of the food chain since we harnessed it. In the old domestic religions of our ancestors, the hearth fire was a God, and it must never be allowed to go out. It was of so much importance to our ancestors that Agamemnon himself, upon returning from the Trojan War, went to his hearth fire FIRST before even sacrificing to Zeus.

Fire is vital to man in every way. His control over fire gave him dominance over nature. It kept him warm and offered comfort in the primitive days of man trying to survive in nature. It became man's ultimate weapon from its earliest forms to the nuclear warhead. Fire is used in the firearms we use to fight with and protect ourselves today. It's owed a particular reverence that we cannot forget. Where Heraclitus believed the world to be ever-living fire, our scientists see the universe as starting with a big bang.

47.

The First Man and Hero

There's a reason we remember a man like Herakles so many thousand years after he's lived. He lived a life that earned him undying fame. It's said that when he died, he was made immortal. What did Herakles do? He fought monsters and made the world safe for mankind. His deeds are so well known that he's present in other cultures. There is belief that Herakles was a protector of The Buddha, for example.

So too, Achilles who showed ARISTEIA. An excellence so unmatched, he's still remembered compared to the multitude of men who have lived since, that we never even knew existed. Move forward to the great conquerors: Alexander the Great, Caesar, Genghis Khan, and Napoleon. This goal of doing something so powerful that mankind has no choice but to remember them is awe-inspiring, but also has within it the potential for great despair. How can you match what these men did? Caesar had such a moment when he turned thirty-three and remembered how much Alexander had conquered as a younger man. Caesar wept over this. The classical man aimed to achieve this kind of undying fame. What would a man have to do in our time to be remembered as we remember Herakles?

It's vital to hold onto this spirit. The spirit of the hero. God has shown that the strong survive and thrive in nature. As long as man strives for superiority, in every way he can, he gives future generations a chance. A great fear expressed by Frank Herbert in his *Dune* novels is the stagnation of mankind. If mankind did not continue to push into new frontiers, test its limits, and grow stronger, nature would sow the seeds of its destruction. Man must continue to adapt to new stress, master new space, and push his limits. Put these things together and you have potential for powerful religion.

What's important to ANY religion is the ability to light the fire in men's souls.

48.

Finding God Through Nature

Ancient Romans thought if you believed in no Gods or just one God, you were an atheist. How can you expect one divine being to be the ultimate creator of everything? They also saw that while the Gods were superior in every way, they still had human-like emotions and faults. They seemed more reasonable in their beliefs of the divine. Our modern society reversed course entirely. There's no chance of there being more than one God and many believe there is no God. Our appearance in the universe is just random chance, according to atheists.

Our enemies often take the position that mankind appeared by random chance as they are facing off against an enemy that believes in the one Almighty God. They have to take this position, though not all do. Friedrich Nietzsche in *Thus Spoke Zarathustra* comments on how a people will make the values of their neighbors bad and the dislikes of their neighbors good. What is good to one people is bad to their neighbors and vice versa. This is how a people separates themselves from everyone else. This belief in one God or no God is the standard of our age while the belief in many Gods — which was the standard of our ancestors — is gone in our time. Those who believe in many Gods, Pagans, have no power and no seat at the table. They aren't even part of the discussion, just weird little sects on the fringes of civilization.

There likely will always be theological debate. It existed even among the Ancient Grek Pagans. A small example of this is

Homer and Heraclitus. The *Iliad* gives an account of the final year of the Trojan War and how The Gods aided in the battles. The Gods are very much "more human than human." Hera, the wife of Zeus, is very much a shafted bride who is trying to stop her husband from sleeping around with whatever female he could stick his dick into. Zeus — the King of the Gods — is not above it all.

Zeus is more powerful than all the other Gods combined, so to stop Zeus and give the Greeks a chance at a critical moment, Hera uses both Aphrodite and Hypnos to lure Zeus into bed with her so that Poseidon can rally the Achaeans. It can't be understated how important a book like Homer's *Iliad* is to not just our people, but all western peoples. It is sacred and a powerful way to learn about true human nature. It may be the REAL Aryan Bible. But can you imagine a Christian thinking about his God as the Greks thought about Zeus? They wouldn't be able to accept that their God was a womanizer or make mistakes. It seems there were Greeks who felt similar. Heraclitus in one of his fragments believed Homer should be whipped.

Heraclitus's work, *On Nature*, was lost to history. We don't know his full thought, but we do know that Heraclitus despised Homer's idea that strife was bad. Strife was vital to life. In one of his fragments, Heraclitus said "War is the Father of all and the King of all." In another, he said "Strife is justice." He also said that wisdom is one only: "It is willing and unwilling to be known by the name of Zeus." Some Greeks had an image of Zeus as the only God that mattered. He was almost seen as the Christian God in this respect.

The other Gods could have been compared to the angels of the Christian God. They simply carried out his will. Heraclitus, however, did not see Zeus as the Almighty Creator. He believed the universe was created by Everliving Fire. Zeus was the creator of man, but not the universe. The *Theogony* took a similar position. Zeus and the Olympians are not the creators of the universe. They overthrew the older Gods who came before them. Moderns look at what the Greeks thought and laugh. Their thought is considered "primitive," but was it not wiser?

We don't know the nature of God. We know a man can is capable of remembering around 150 people. What are the limits of God's power? The Greks and Romans, perhaps rightfully, concluded that there couldn't be only one God. The universe is unknowably complex. There are likely many Gods making the world turn.

These debates almost always break down into bitter arguments between Christians and Pagans. For Pagans, their rites and complete beliefs are lost to history. Much of their theology owes its survival to Christians. How do you know the Christians didn't change something? Christians still understand their theology, but almost all the practitioners of the modern age have been corrupted by the new faith of leftism. Yes, you say Christianity is the truth. But how come Christianity is being scraped off the world stage? How is it losing its power? The Christian seems to hate the Pagan more than the leftist who is actually conquering his faith.

The new faith, leftism, is Christianity without God. It has made science the new priesthood and blacks the new saints. This is, however, only one flavor of atheism. Nietzsche too, put forth a new atheistic faith. One that went onwards and upwards. Nietzsche made the diagnosis that God was already dead in his time. That man had killed him and the only way for man to come to terms with his crime was to become a God himself. To make himself worthy of the crime.

Nietzsche's philosophy isn't for everybody. Jonathan Bowden believed it was "too harsh and forbidding" for most people. Nietzsche had vision that man had to become higher than himself. He had to become more. He had to become an overman, a beyond-man. Doing this involved taking a view of life that was LIFE-AFFIRMING. A view that life itself was the Will to Power. It was the accumulation of forces and power. To not just survive but thrive.

There is value to be found in almost all these different beliefs. I believe the Nietzschean ideal is the best course into the future. To orient a people towards the Will to Power is the right path. Where I believe Nietzsche to be wrong, however, is in his assertion that God is dead. God is not dead, we have not killed him. God is UNKNOWABLE because we have strayed too far from the doctrines of nature, too far from His Golden Path. But you should not hold Nietzsche's words on God against him. It cannot be denied that Nietzsche was a man God spoke to.

There are billions of people. It's naive to believe there is only one divinity influencing mankind. It may be wiser to believe many Gods and demons are influencing the affairs of mankind. Perhaps, each race has its own God. Whether there is one God, or many Gods isn't the right question. The right question is WHY isn't mankind being influenced by God today? God isn't dead, but he has seemingly left mankind to its fate.

If mankind can get itself back onto the Golden Path, God will be known again. What we suffer through today is perhaps, punishment from God. In the Bible, God destroyed Sodom and Gomorrah for their degeneracy. Perhaps, he has left us to our fate for our own. Are we to become some failed experiment or will we redeem the race?

49.

The problems of our time stem from our enemies' desire to liberate themselves from nature. Our enemies represent the army of the deformed. Modern peoples, in their arrogance, believe that mankind has surpassed nature. "You can't be racist because we don't need racism anymore. We know that people are mostly the same." You don't have to be in shape anymore because you don't have to hunt for food, you can just go to the supermarket. All your ailments can be cured with a pill, no need to take preventative measures.

They want to make themselves different from their neighbors who they see as the White Man and all his supposed evils such as the Nazi regime in Germany or the American's history of slavery. They will consciously make themselves the opposite of what they see as the "great evil." This course, however, moves our people away from the Golden Path and puts us in the precarious position of being anti-life and anti-nature. They see the ways of our forefathers as backwards and bigoted instead of virtues of survival and the lessons learned over time. This path is folly for many reasons. Nature isn't kind. It isn't anti-racist or anything close to that. What's got us to this point is the Way of the Fathers and their lessons learned which were passed down to us through religious rites and stern old traditions.

The reason we no longer know God is because we have strayed from His Golden Path. We refuted the Way of the Fathers in favor of "science." Now there is nothing inherently wrong with science. It will be a vital tool in the future, but it is not the religion it's made out to be by our enemies. Science is not beyond greed and corruption. True science affirms the Way of the Fathers every time. Quack science can't figure out if an egg is healthy or not and affirms mental illnesses such as transgenderism.

Every religion claims to know the truth and the way and at certain times in history, I believe they were right. They all, however, lost the path and when they lost the path, it was because they abandoned the true way of God. The truth and the way aren't found in religious rites and documents, it's found in natural law. In the doctrines of nature. When the old religions flourished, it was because the people were keenly aware of the doctrines of nature. They may not have known the doctrines or were consciously aware of them, but they acted in accordance with nature. God in turn gave them favor. He loved them. And it is a goal of a people to be loved by God.

An argument you will find in the Pagan and Nietzschean sects is that you have to live according to nature. The Pagans believe The Gods are a part of nature. Christianity at it its strongest point was living in accordance with nature. Nietzscheans rightly see the doctrines of nature as the law of the universe. It doesn't matter the specifics of the religion or its texts, when a people live as they were meant to, they dominate. The doctrines of nature are the way of God. It boggles the mind how a man can claim God created the universe but preach religious rites that run contrary to nature.

If God created the world, the doctrines of nature are the way of God. The truth, the true faith, can only be found in the doctrines of nature. When man embarks on the Golden Path. This is how a people can be loved by God again. If you want to know God again, you must live in accordance with nature. The doctrines of nature aren't kind, they don't care about equality, or "marginalized" groups, and it only cares about one thing above all else: victory. If you can't win, if you can't get to the top, your ideas mean nothing.

In the words of Ragnar Redbeard: Might is Right. Not only is might is right but might makes right. Victory sanctifies every cause. This is the way of the world; this is the way of God. It's apparent in every great empire and people. You have to strive again to become superior. To not get caught in the weeds of pointless ethnic strife and racial guilt.

50.

It's naïve to believe there is no God. We know God is out there for we have seen what happens to the godless. They forget what it means to be human. They forsake our Fathers. Forsake all the natural instincts that got us to where we are today. They are easily manipulated by very bad people to act against their own interests and the interests of their race. They've bought into the idea of individualism to the extreme, at the cost of all other bonds. There is only one natural course to this path.

The godless have no higher purpose to live for. To believe in no God is tantamount to despair. Man has a higher purpose and to know this purpose is give him power. Power to overcome all obstacles. Their despair is rancid. It comes out in how they look, how they smell, and gives way to grotesque deformities.

You must harden yourself against such godlessness. The faithful will find their way back to God again when we return to the Golden Path.

51.

You will often find groups that should be aligned in opposition to the prevailing religion fighting each other. Christians and Pagans are always at odds. There are arguments to be made about both. The Pagan may say the Christian has forgotten his place in nature. The Christian will make a call back to the Christian conquest of Paganism. Paganism itself is a small minority and this group is also separated into the many different Pagan religions.

The differences between the religions is likely LESS important than the similarities. The similarities will likely move our people closer to the Golden Path. They are pieces of human nature and the way. I mentioned before the similarities between Christianity and Greek Paganism. Zeus and the Christian God both are the strongest. Do the Olympians share the same role of Angels in Christian mythology? No, the Christians didn't perform sacrifices, but the organization of the pantheons is similar.

The similarities are even greater between Aryan religions. You can gain a greater knowledge of the Way of the Fathers by noting these similarities. The differences likely come from their time apart from the other peoples as well as their experiences in their different homelands. What matters most is learning from the lessons of our fathers. Piecing together the Way of the Fathers and orienting our people toward the next frontier. It's on the frontier that we experience nature in its rawest form and it is by nature that we learn how to become strong again.

52.

The Nature of God

The society in which we are born is godless, but it is not without religion. Our enemies have risen false idols to take the place of God. We have, in turn, become unworthy of God and it shows in the state of our society. When you turn from the path of God, He — through nature — sows the seeds of your destruction. He created man for a purpose. God selects for the right type of man through the process we call nature. The way back to God, to know God again, is through religion, but not just any religion, a Warrior Religion.

Our enemies decry religion while practicing their own abomination of it. True religion is not what you hear professed in the mainstream today. The mainstream seeks liberation from nature. They are anti-life and anti-nature. They poison the blood nature of man. Make his body sick and frail. This is a religion of the sick and malformed, trying with all its might to drag man into hell with them.

True religion is life-affirming. It awakens within you what you already know in the blood. All men seek to be enlightened. Religion is the most honorable path to this enlightenment. Religion is a piece of human nature. For the thousands of years man has existed, religion has guided men into the future. It's only in recent times that it's been used to the detriment of the people it's tasked with guiding.

How many religions have come and gone throughout human history? No man can say. The ones we know of were very much part of the nature of its people. Even the Aryans who made their way out of the Balkans saw their religions diversify the further they moved away from the point of origin. You can certainly find similarities between them, but the land left its mark upon them. Their different situations led to different ends. Their Gods changed. The lessons they learned were remembered in the religion to guide their children in the future.

Those who won, who achieved their paradise in life, paid a heavy price for victory. They got soft, they lost their edge. While they likely did not pay this toll in their lifetimes, their descendants would. It's important to avoid this selfishness. You must think about all the men who came before you as well as the ones who will come after you. Man is engaged in the true struggle: the fight for survival. The fight for survival is a matter that concerns all men. No matter how easy you think your life is now in comparison to your ancestors, you must not forget that the war rages into eternity.

What is it that made our ancestors go soft and lose their edge? Was it getting comfortable? Civilization building? Perhaps. This universe is God's and through nature, we can glimpse his designs for man. Nature selects for the strong. We know this in the bones. As Oswald Spengler said, "Human history is war history." We remember only the conquerors out of the multitudes of people who have existed.

What's most important for you to remember is the universe cannot go backwards. There is no returning to some better time. You can only go forward into the unknown. God favors the ones that do. Who would have realized how quickly Americans spread from "sea to shining sea" in their quest for Manifest Destiny? Each time you're able to move your tribe further into the frontier, it grows in VITAL FORCE, but it is also forever changed by the land it takes. The frontier will always create a new type of man.

53.

A marker of religion is the reliance on divinity. A Warrior Religion rejects this reliance. You saw it in the Pagan religions where men looked for omens from their Gods to shed light on a decision before them. This practice was at least more honest compared to what's happened more recently. The Pagans understood that God had decided not to favor them on some particular day. The Romans used to say, "I give, so that You may give." It was a contractual agreement between the Romans and their Gods. Whenever it didn't work out in their favor, they had to go through the rites and try to figure out what they did wrong.

In Christianity, as seen in the Book of Job, God didn't answer your prayers. He had a plan for you. For good or for ill was his business. Your duty was to remain faithful. To accept Christ in your heart. Ask for forgiveness. Paradise was not of this world.

This mentality turned against Christians. The ability to have your sins forgiven by asking for forgiveness was an excuse to become grotesque. You could ask for forgiveness later. Their ancestors understood that it wasn't that easy. Your life has to be pious. The actions you committed would be held over your head by the Lord.

A Warrior Religion should prefer a Buddhistic approach. You must be responsible for yourself. Life is war and war calls you back to life. Misfortune happens to us all, at varying intensities. Your worth as a man depends on your ability to overcome your misfortune and impose your will. Do not blame God for the punishment you reap on yourself. It's not God's fault if you mistreat and disfigure your soul.

A man's life upon the earth is warfare. You must stand strong, have courage, and overcome, against all odds. Fate is the same for everyone. We're all going to die. You must bring honor to your name and bloodline. Act in service to your tribe. It's important to remember that the strength and survival of the tribe come above all else.

The rampant, absolute individualism of modern society has fractured all bonds of fellowship between men. Individualism is a piece of human nature, but not in the extreme. Not at the cost of the whole. When this is allowed, bad actors worm their way in like parasites to suck the life out of a people. Better to calm your heart of such selfishness. Be of service to the tribe and the tribe's greatness. Superiority must be proven.

Take responsibility for what befalls you. Overcome it. Master it. Step over and beyond it, further into this battle we call life.

54.

The fire of God must be unleashed.

Maintain the strength of God. This universe is His and we must navigate the path he's laid out to us. Is He the only God? I do not know. I'm inclined to say no, but he is OUR God. We are chosen by Him.

The Great Work before us is Manifest Destiny, but on a scale not yet seen upon this earth. But it can't stop there, we must move beyond the earth. Man is vulnerable on Earth. All his eggs in one basket. We seek the stars. But before we can focus on the heavens, we must first conquer our enemies around us and set the foundation.

55.

"Civilizations collapse when their powers outrun their religions!" -Frank Herbert

The biggest problem our people face today is a civilization whose power has outrun the religion they were born out of. Frank Herbert, the author of the *Dune* series believed this event led to civilizational collapse. We are seeing this today. The enemy maintains the morality of Christianity but has rejected the religion. What we've seen happen to Christianity is likely what happened to the many Pagan religions during Christianity's rise to power. The power of these peoples far passed the ends of the religion they were born out of. Its priests could not fathom just how far their tribe would reach out into the frontier.

This reaching out, this Will to Power, is a cornerstone of a Warrior Religion. We recognize what it is God selects for in man. We will reach into the unknown, strive to do what no one else has done before, in our quest to become worthy of God again.

56.

What is the nature of God?

Every religion claims to know the truth. A new Warrior Religion should make no such claim. We know that we don't know. Is God a child at play as suggested by the Grek philosopher, Heraclitus? Is he just moving pieces on a board game? Perhaps, God is trying to move His chosen people toward the Golden Path or maybe he doesn't care at all? Maybe God is long gone, in some other universe creating new life. God may be like a scientist, trying to figure out the perfect alchemy for life. We don't know.

What we do know is that different peoples have peaked at different times in human history. These peoples had different religions, but they all turned the wheel of mankind. There is much IRE between Christians and Pagans, but both have at one time, been seemingly chosen by God for the Great Work. This leaves one to question, how? Perhaps, it's not necessarily the religion that provides the disciple with the truth, rather it is something else entirely. There is a way of God hidden in nature and the peoples that can rise to the top of the food chain are unknowingly following this path. It would be the mission of a Warrior Religion to get our people back on this path.

57.

All men seek to be enlightened. Religion is the most ancient and honorable way men try to make sense of their world. This feeling is just as present now than in any other time even though the traditional religions appear to be on the ropes. What are you on this earth for? What are you meant to do? What is the purpose of life? All religions have tried to answer this question.

For the Pagans, religion was means of working out deals with The Gods to ensure their survival and victory in wars. These men were closer to the primitive, to the darkness. Some peoples have come and gone without us ever knowing about them. Whose stories are lost to time. They saw their relationship with the Gods as contractual. Perform the ritual in the right manner and The Gods will aid them. If this didn't turn out the way they wanted it to, the priests would look over the ritual and try to figure out what went wrong, what omen was missed.

In a way, I believe the early Pagans were less confused about the purpose of life and enlightenment than any other era. Life at its core is about the fight for survival and the mastery of space. It's about strength, nature, and blood. Seeing just how far into the frontier man is meant to go. The Pagans, so close to nature in its rawest form, worked to master space and the conditions they were born into. It was about securing a home for future generations so that they wouldn't have to suffer in the wild as they did. Making their tribe more powerful on the world stage so none would test their supremacy.

Our culture is extremely individualistic compared to Pagan cultures. It's not that the Pagans didn't have individualism, but the survival of the tribe was paramount to all else. They had to work together to make it happen and you see this in their religions which at the beginning was very decentralized. Each family had its own Gods and religion. Oftentimes, the ancestors were their Gods. The hearth fire was a sacred God. Over time, they added city Gods and adopted foreign Gods. A city could have three Gods named Herakles. Eventually, they realized those multiple Herakles were likely all the same God.

What was enlightenment for the Pagans? In a way, MIGHT IS RIGHT. Xenophon on speaking to the Ten Thousand before their up-country march said, *"If any of you has set his heart on seeing his friends again, let him remember to prove himself a man; there is no other way to achieve his heart's wish. Or is mere living an object with any of you, strive to conquer; if to slay is the privilege of victory, to die is the doom of the defeated."* Conquerors kill and the conquered die. Many warriors sought to achieve ataraxia in battle. Ataraxia meant total calmness, similar to the Buddhist nirvana.

They saw ataraxia as a means to battle fury. Ancient meant sought to leave their mark on the world, to obtain undying fame. You could only do this by excelling above all others on the battlefield. To be like Herakles or Achilles. If you can get immortal glory, you will become a God. This is what appealed to the Greeks. To be the best.

The Romans, while similar, had a different concept. After a bad loss early in its history, Romans made a vow to never admit defeat in war. *"The enemy is not vanquished if he does not believe himself so,"* was a quote from Ennius and a saying for the Roman martial character. You can make the argument that the Romans were the manliest people to ever walk the earth. They didn't believe in hiding their faults. Every scar or ugly feature was shown to the world. This was who they were and wanted you to take their best shot at them.

Labor was of immense importance to the Roman. His animus — the Roman conception of the soul — had to always be in motion. Directed toward a higher goal. An inert animus was a sign of cowardice. Legionaries were half warriors, half construction workers, building fortresses overnight in enemy territories. The Romans often found themselves at odds with bigger and stronger barbarian tribes. Their will to win and extreme martial discipline made them an empire that every country since has tried to emulate.

What was enlightenment for the Romans? It was the exercising of one's will. It was to show that every action you made was done by your own will. The American likes to see a man overcome all odds to achieve victory. He wants to see the underdog come out on top. This didn't move the Romans. What moved the Romans was the recapturing of lost honor. Lucretia taking her own life after being raped. The defeated gladiator presenting his neck to be cut. The child of Hector choosing to throw himself off the wall of Troy rather than be killed by the Greeks. Defiant to the end.

58.

Now you must understand that this discussion of enlightenment and what it meant to embody the spirit of a race was for culture in its spring, to use Oswald Spengler's terminology. When their cultures devolved into civilizations, the character and spirit of the people changed. No longer were they living instinctively, in the moment. The people yearned to be like their ancestors. Greek philosophy came about in their civilization phase as their philosophers tried to figure out what went wrong with their society. When their culture died, they left behind Platonism as its spiritual residue. In our modern times, the worship of Platonism over Greek vitalism may be a sign of our decline. Perhaps, our academics share a kinship with the Greek philosophers.

You saw the decline of Roman culture in the rise of the Stoics. Men who couldn't change what was happening around them. The height of empire and the rise of Christianity left them with no other way to cope than to adopt the attitude of the stoic. The spiritual residue of the Romans was Christianity. Christianity made quick work of a Roman culture already on the ropes and transformed into a powerhouse when it fused with the Germanic warrior ethos in the early medieval period. You can argue when and where the Pagans were converted, but it wasn't as early as when the Christians claimed they were. Christians owe what vitality they had to the Germanic tribes.

Christianity and Buddhism take different paths to enlightenment. Christianity turned an honor and shame culture into a guilt culture and strove for aestheticism. In the past, if a man committed a crime but wasn't caught, it was no skin off his back because his tribe didn't know. He couldn't be dishonored. Christianity changed this by putting in him the idea that while his people didn't know his crime, God did. What do you think about this? Did the priest who proclaimed God saw all do so because he truly believed this to be true or was it a means of controlling a people when they didn't have the force to?

Some Christians still hold fast to the doctrines of nature. I do not mean to attack them. They are men of race. The poet Robinson Jeffers recognized the greatness of such men when he said that Western greatness is in part due to the discordance of such a man's spirituality. He unconsciously is trying to settle his innate Pagan virtues with his Christian conversion. Since he cannot easily do this, the discordance causes him to impose his will on what he can master and control: the world around him.

The vast majority, however, have had their right natures subverted by Christianity. The technological improvement of mankind has allowed them to blossom throughout society and give birth to new, more dangerous ideologies. Christianity and all its offshoots seek to liberate themselves from nature. If you refer to Nietzsche's *On The Genealogy of Morals*, he has an entire section devoted to Christianity. Christianity, you see, is not the natural religion of our ancestors. It was imposed upon them by conversion. While Jews and Christians don't get along today, and the Christianity of Europeans during the early medieval period was nothing like Christianity as it exists today, Christianity itself was born from Judea. Nietzsche makes the argument that the last thousand years have been the battle between Rome and Judea, a battle won by the latter.

Now, was Christianity made to subvert the Romans and all the other Westerners who adopted it? Certainly, there are believers in the idea that this has been a two-thousand-year conspiracy on part of the Jews to exact revenge on their persecution at the hands of the Romans. Medieval Germanic tribes all tried to keep the Jews out of their societies, believing they would destroy them. I believe this is the wrong way to think about Christianity and the Jews. It creates a victim mindset and claiming victimization will do nothing to save you

91

as the system itself was made to destroy you. Rather, you should respect Jewish tribalism and recognize what a people can do when it becomes clannish to the extreme. It's something you must manifest in your own people.

Enlightenment isn't so much a question for the Christian, it's forgiveness of sin. He seeks forgiveness before Christ. To save as many souls as he can. To get his soul into heaven. Hell, he must save mankind by converting them all to Christianity. This is his enlightenment. Now I don't expect to dissuade Christians from their religion, only to push them back towards their spiritual discordance and the remembrance that there are virtues necessary for the survival of a people.

I believe the doctrines of nature are the ways of God and while I don't share the belief in Christ, I hope that a Christian can see the wisdom in those words. Wisdom that his people have followed for centuries. Their desire to convert mankind to the Christian faith was in accordance with nature.

59.

Buddhism is a different animal entirely. The goal of its religion is enlightenment, nirvana. It's suspected that Jesus Christ studied in India during his lifetime and brought their teaching back to Rome. I believe the way of Buddhism is noble, but at its core, it's a rejection of life. It's a rejection of strength, nature, and blood. But it's a rejection out of love. The Buddhist loves all life, and he doesn't want to see life suffer.

The Buddhist understands that all life is suffering and does his part to reduce suffering. He will give up all desires to do this. This path, while noble, rejects the biological imperative of mankind. It's resigning to death. Buddhism in the extreme is a kill signal to a people. You may gain enlightenment, but at what cost?

There is a strand of Buddhism that is important to mankind and the idea of enlightenment, however. This strand gives strength to man as he confronts life. It's the idea that you shouldn't curse God for the punishment you inflict upon yourself. The universe is God's. He's laid it out according to his own designs and it's up to man to find His golden path. The Buddhistic understanding of suffering is key to this path. Paradise is NOT heaven. Leftism tries to make heaven on earth and it's nothing but a hell. Paradise is the frontier and the fight for survival in nature.

60.

What should a Warrior Religion think about enlightenment? Enlightenment is the process in which man discovers the way of God through His Golden Path. What is it that makes a people great? What is it that ensures our survival as a species? What does nature select for? The answer to these questions is enlightenment. As Heraclitus said, "The way of man has no wisdom, but the way of God does."

Strength, nature, and blood are the keys to the equation, the frontier, and the Golden Path. We may not know the destination God has for us or the purpose behind it. It's not our place to know just yet. What's important to understand is that failure to stay on God's Golden Path leads to stagnation and stagnation is the kill signal of a species.

Take the earth, for example. We are born from the earth. It is our home, but we have shown the potential to leave Earth. We know through science that the earth can be destroyed in a myriad of ways. Remaining on earth is the equivalent of keeping all your eggs in one basket. If mankind wants to survive, it must move beyond the earth. This is the way of God.

61.

Religious Discordance of Western Man

There is always strife between Christians and Pagans. Christians generally can't understand the gall of people choosing to worship religions they already conquered while Pagans blame Christians for the state of the modern world. I do my best to show respect to both sides because neither one is the enemy. We are united in the fight for survival against the real enemy: leftism. There are pros and cons on each side. It's not as set in stone as either would have you believe. Christianity may have destroyed the Pagan belief structure, but leftism has done the same to Christianity in turn. Both religions are spiraling the toilet bowl.

This is where I want to make the point that Christianity — in all likelihood — was designed specifically to destroy Paganism. It came out of a people who despised everything about the Romans. By the same token, the enemy's religion was designed specifically to destroy Christianity. Do you understand what this means? It means you cannot use Paganism or Christianity to conquer this new foe. They have you figured out and will dominate you on every battlefield. The belief structures that gave these religions vital force in the past were figured out.

Resistance against the enemy fails because we don't understand their belief structure. They have the initiative in every battle, bettering their odds of victory in any engagement. Now it may be an impossible task to ask either the Christian or Pagan to abandon their belief structure to take a path better oriented towards victory, but I will reconcile Christianity with Paganism and offer a new path.

62.

Modern Americans have been reduced to the signifier, "White people." This subversive language helped to erase the

American's understanding of who he is and where he comes from. There was a study done in the 1970s that showed there were seventeen different White ethnic groups in America. How much of these tribes' histories, customs, and traditions have been lost to time? I encourage you, if you haven't already, to learn about your ancestral heritage. My mother's paternal line is linked to the Mayflower while my father's to America's martial mountain peoples: the Scots-Irish, arriving in the New World in the 1730s. The leftist "academic" bullshit they indoctrinate Americans with is the idea that RACE doesn't matter.

We don't know the extent that race matters, but rest assured, it's much more than just skin color. The reason I bring this up is because I feel a powerful kinship between those who share my heritage. It may be a matter of the language and values we share; it may have to do with the kinship of the race. I feel that the issue of our time, in a way, has been figured out and it's been figured out by a fellow Scots-Irish American. A poet by the name of Robinson Jeffers. Jeffers was amongst the first settlers of a virginal California — long before it became what it was today. He was considered a genius in his youth, speaking six languages, and was accepted into university at the age of fifteen.

He was raised under Scots-Irish Calvinism, but he "rejected the Christ at fifteen," as said by Jonathan Bowden in a speech he did on the poet. This was at a time when Christianity was the dominant religion in the country. Jeffers believed in some of the bedrock values of what it meant to be American. Like most Scots-Irish, he believed that you shouldn't have to call the state to deal with your problems. You dealt with them yourself. Life to Jeffers wasn't the Christian good vs evil, it was about the fight for survival.

In a biography published about Jeffers called *The Stone Mason of Tor House* by Melba Berry Bennet, there are very interesting thoughts from Jeffers about religion and Western Man. Jeffers claims that the greatness of Western Man stems from an unresolved conflict in his mind between his Christian conversion and his innate Pagan virtues. What did Jeffers mean by this? He saw virtues like justice, vengeance, pride, personal honor, Will to Power, and patriotism as descending from Paganism. These virtues were ingrained into the psyche of Westerners. Christianity wasn't something native to him, it was imposed upon him through conversion. He's accepted this conversion and all the Christian values it entails like piety, universal love, humility, and non-resistance.

The two competing value systems — the Pagan Virtues vs Christian Virtues — created a religious discordance in Western man's soul and this discordance is what made him great. Our minds are trying to settle the difference in values. You can say our body pulls towards the more primordial Pagan virtues while our Christian mind tries to settle the difference in feelings. Since Western men cannot settle these differences, the conflict is unresolved. Jeffers says *"A person who is not at peace inwardly is the more likely to be active outwardly. And a person who cannot subdue himself will be driven to subdue others."* With this, can you see how Western man has conquered the world? How has he arrived at the top of the food chain?

I believe in a way, this same conflict still exists in the mind of the enemy, where our side hasn't resolved it, but so much time has passed that the Pagan virtues are fading in their strength on us. When you start talking Christian vs Pagan, the fire arises in the Christian, but he only knows how to "crush" the Pagan.

63.

Robinson Jeffers's observation on the religious discordance of Western man is the key to dominating the enemy and revitalizing our people. The religious discordance is simmering out in our time as Christian values are accepted "in the blood," so to speak. We — as a society — have found temporary liberation from the demands of nature. Of course, it's impossible to liberate mankind completely from nature. We are eternally bound to it. The longer we accept this comfort, the more dangerous the future becomes. If we are made too soft, if we stagnate too long, God will sow the seeds of our destruction.

The way of God is natural law. To stray from this path is to stray from God. In a way, the virtues Jeffers referred to are not Pagan virtues. Certainly, they were adopted by Paganism, but they are not Pagan virtues, they are the virtues of survival. Of mankind's fight for survival in nature. These virtues are PRIMORDIAL. They existed long before Paganism. Paganism adopted them to survive, but once they got comfortable and lost their edge, Christianity took the reins.

What must be done is to recreate Jeffers' religious discordance but in reverse. You must take Western man with his Christian values and impose upon him Pagan conversion. Now do not take offense, one way or the other, to my usage of Christian and Pagan. Christian values HAVE disseminated to man on a societal level. The enemy proclaims to hate Christians while accepting their value system and morality. To put it differently, you have to teach man the virtues of survival again. And then, let the natural contradictions with Christianity play out as they will. You will create a new religious discord in the mind of your people and be able to harness a power the enemy doesn't understand.

You don't have to abandon Christianity or Paganism to do this. You only have to convert mankind to these virtues of survival, at all costs, for the survival of the species. HELL is the extinction of mankind. HEAVEN is the next frontier. The fight for survival affects us all. The Pagan virtues discussed above are really Primordial Virtues primitive man learned to survive and thrive in nature.

Don't get caught up in the fight between Christianity and Paganism, it's irrelevant next to the fight for survival. Paganism likely didn't invent the "Pagan" virtues, they were around before the religions as we know them today. You will only run into problems if you can't take these virtues of survival and adapt them to your religion — if you choose a path that involves creating a new denomination for your faith. A new Warrior Religion should believe God is unknowable to modern man as we've strayed too far from his path. Whether he's one God or many isn't known, nor is it our concern. We believe he is a WAR GOD for his preference of superior, martial peoples, but our primary concern is getting back on the path and avoiding the stagnation of mankind, the death signal of a species.

Our virtues are the virtues of survival. The Primordial Virtues. The sense of justice, of taking vengeance against our enemies, pride, personal honor, the Will to Power, and patriotic duty to fight for your people. A Christian might take issue with say the desire for vengeance, but framing matters above all else. What, so a Christian shouldn't fight back against someone bullying him? Maybe this new type of Christian, but the real Christians understand that evil(that which is trying to destroy you) must be destroyed. Christianity for a long time was on the path of God, following he doctrines of nature. It's only in recent times that it's hit roadblocks and lost the way.

64.

When I talk about CONVERSION in a Warrior Religion, I talk about getting your race, your people, back on the path of God. What does this mean to the disciple? You want your tribe focused on strength and survival. And then, towards the ideals of power and excellence. GOD rewards the people who find a way to not only survive but thrive in nature. The name of the game is excellence. It's domination. It's pushing your people into the frontier, into discomfort, where you're forced to adapt and hone your craft. Life ain't meant to be comfortable.

Comfort leads to stagnation and stagnation is the kill signal. This is why you see lines of Kings fail. They end up losing their edge after generations of pure comfort and paradise. The satisfaction you get from mastering new space, that is the real the paradise.

PART THREE:
WARRIOR RELIGION

65.

War as Father

It's said in the Greek theogony that everything sprang forth from Chaos. From Chaos, you get Gaia the Earth who then gives birth to Ouranos the Sky. It's through the copulation between Sky and Earth that we get the Titans. Kronos, the youngest Titan, castrated Ouranos to separate heaven and earth. He is the father many of the Olympians, who Zeus overthrows to become King of The Gods. Through the pairing of Zeus and his sister Hera is Ares, the God of War. It's rumored perhaps, the Greek theogony is inspired by the Greeks conquering the aboriginals and merging their two pantheons. The Titans represent residual of conquest. The question that arises is how you settle the theogony with important Heraclitus fragment, "War is the Father of all and King of all; some he has shown to be gods and others men, some slaves and some free."

War itself is actually considered to be a daemon, a divine embodiment, by the Ancient Greeks. If you look back to the primordial development of mankind, you realize that War is much older than The Gods. I don't claim to know the divine theogony, but when the first creations of man are stone and wood technology, before even fire. All those before the development of language, you realize that War is perhaps, extremely important to man. The first men you see, were engaged in the true struggle in its rawest form. War finds himself King, being the first and ultimate trade of man. To make it in this world, you have to fight.

There is a cliché expression that we stand on the shoulders of giants, and this is true. The first men had to deal with prehistoric beasts and other species of man in their fight for survival. In this struggle, they weren't the strongest, but they became the most skilled at WAR. Before any of the modern developments of mankind, some men figured out how to use stone and wood to make spears, axes, and the like. In their fight for survival, they had to learn to excel at and master the ultimate trade. They had to think outside the box to win, their ingenuity was a virtue in this time as it still is today.

What the first men discovered is a primordial liking for war. As Oswald Spengler tells us: "human history is war history." No matter how much leftists wail against this, you can't change it. We tell our history by the battles and wars that took place. By the great men and conquerors. Not by anything else. This is the standard of mankind. It's how we judge nations, peoples, and men. How well can they make war? What Great Works have they accomplished through war?

66.
"War was always here. Before man, war waited for him. The ultimate trade awaiting its ultimate practitioner." -Judge Holden in Cormac McCarthy's *Blood Meridian*

It doesn't matter what you think of War, War is.

Is this what Heraclitus meant by War being the Father of all? Is War the true Father of man? Did the Greeks get it wrong? Perhaps, the Christians were closer to the truth in their own Genesis story: "In the beginning was the Word, and the Word was with God, and the Word was God." The God of the Old Testament comes off as this MIGHT IS RIGHT deity, perhaps his true name is WAR. The height of Christianity is its medieval period and The Holy Roman Empire. A period marked by WAR and Crusades. Real Christians yearn to RETVRN to the Knights Templar.

Could it be at the real meaning behind the Book of JOB was to be MIGHTY? To excel at War. For if you don't, you let yourself get trampled over by the strong. The lesson of the Father is War. To be the mightiest! A man or race's ability to do this determines the mark they will leave on the world. How they will be remembered by history.

We don't remember the weak. We remember men like Alexander the Great or Julius Caesar. History will not remember the plight of the left in our time if they do not defeat countries on the field of battle. Our enemies aren't on the "right side of history," they are hanging on the coattails of American greatness and history will remember them as such. This sounds mean like we hold disdain for the weak and pacifists, but these traits aren't selected for in nature. Will there be people born with wrong natures? Yes, and they must play a part in society. It's a mistake, however, to worship them like Gods.

The worship of the wrong natures pushes a culture to the brink. Man senses it's wrong in the blood and when he doesn't, his mind reminds him through ailments such as depression and sickness. There is reason men get adrenaline and endorphin release while partaking in physical culture. They are doing what they're meant to do. They're showing the right nature and the ancient DNA in the body reaffirms this.

67.

The right nature to have towards War is that it doesn't matter whether you like it, you must strive for excellence in war regardless of your feelings toward it.

The survival of your people in the true struggle depends on your ability to excel in war. Martial excellence. The Ancient Greeks loathed Ares, but they also had to endure great and terrible hardships in their lives because of the consequences of war. Despite this, they were good enough at war that we still admire them today. We have given the Spartans immortal fame for their stand at Thermopylae. The Spartans themselves believed they were descended from the demigod Herakles who himself, is a hero who's passed through the ages. And we remember them precisely because of his martial excellence.

The right nature is the one that honors War as Father. Not only because it ensures the survival of our people, but it's in our blood. We were selected for our ability to wage war. The ultimate trade for the ultimate practitioner. There is a reason mankind became the ultimate disciples of War. His bloodied sword guides us toward some greater purpose.

Where the Ancient Greeks despised War, the Romans revered him. They did not have the kind of flash and finesse of the Greeks at the time. They were a manly and warlike people facing threats on their borders. They saw the world through War. This is the better attitude to take and the reason why the Roman Empire lasted so long. When you can orient your people toward the doctrines of nature, they will last as long as they can keep to it. War will guide the willing and annihilate the unwilling.

Honor War as God and you will lead your people to victory and salvation. Why wouldn't the warrior worship War? And by extension, a Warrior Religion. It's not just the warriors that call on War, but the mechanics, technicians, scientists, and doctors that make modern war what it is. It's through War and victory in war that a people survive. The fight for survival holds us together.

"War is my god." -James LaFond

68.

Friedrich Nietzsche makes the argument in his first essay in *On The Genealogy of Morals*, that the struggle of the last thousand years was the morality of Judea vs Rome. The Roman, aristocratic morality, defined as good equals noble, mighty, beautiful, and loved by God, vs Judea, the slave morality, defined as good equals the poor, pious, weak, and lowly. You don't have to read Nietzsche to know that Judea won out in our time. Even leftism — which has put Christianity in its iron sights — bases itself on the same morality. The most popular religions in the world share, with small variations, similar moral systems.

Everything we know is this Christian morality. Everything in our world derives from it. As society has degraded and moved closer to Spengler's Decline, we've separated the people from the origins of their morality. Leftists kept the fanaticism but left behind the value system. This turned the left into a wrecking ball to be used against their enemies. They have no origin, no grounding, and can be manipulated to fight for whatever cause becomes the flavor of the month for their masters.

You may ask why the origin matters. It's not enough to just be opposed to something, you have to be *for* an alternative. Propose a superior way, otherwise, you get swept up in the minutiae of the news outrage cycle. You must have PURPOSE. You must know what you're fighting for, not just what you're fighting against. This has been a major problem on our side as wretched people get brought up as opposition to the enemy, only to find out they're just as bad or one step removed from what you're fighting against. Thou shalt not worship false gods.

Nietzsche wanted to see a return to aristocratic morality where "good = noble = mighty = beautiful = loved by God" and this is excellent starting point. In some ways, the right has done this. There's much support for men trying to be strong and healthy in this sphere. You must go out of your way to support strength and beauty where you see it. Applaud true heroism and nobility where you see it. Encourage men to form their own mannerbunds again. This is where the alternative forms by distinguishing what's good from bad.

The left gets its fanaticism and morality from the Christian Crusader. They see their cause as righteous; they're safeguarding the helpless from "demonic" racists and bigots. They see the world through the eyes of Christian dualism: good and evil. You don't just have a different view from them, you hold morally evil views that are a danger to mankind. It's their moral duty to not just oppose you but to destroy you. This is something the normie on our side doesn't understand. You can't reason with them; they don't even see you as human.

If you want to "oppose" this, your foundations must be strong. You must have greater devotion and fanaticism then to your enemies. You have to be willing to fight. To show the enemy no mercy. For some, however, it's not enough to just know the enemy wants to destroy them. I cannot say why, maybe they're in denial over the course of events. What I want to do is provide superior belief structures. Something worth fighting for. Worth dying for.

69.

"Just as the primeval forest strives ever more toweringly and mightily to the heights, sucking its growth forces from its own decline, so each new human generation grows on soil made stratified by the decomposition of countless generations that now rest here from the circle of life." -Ernst Jünger

The Way of the Fathers

This belief structure I have named The Way of the Fathers represents a fusion of two different thinkers: Nietzsche's idea of the Will to Power with Ernst Jünger's Warrior Mysticism. I've spoken on the importance of bloodline in the prior chapter, **The Sacred Fire**. Jünger provides a powerful foundation to the Sacred Fire. In his short book, *War as Inner Experience*, he dives into his upbringing in the Reich and the blood and soil belief structure of the Germans. The Germans were grounded into the land they carved out for themselves. For Jünger, the German people represented a "primeval forest."

In The Sacred Fire, I spoke about the ancient family. How they saw FIRE as a representation of their bloodline and each patriarch had a duty to keep their fire going. The hearth fire in the ancient home was a deity. Each family had their own Gods. Each family was charged with feeding their dead ancestors after they passed. For a woman to marry a man, she had — through ritual — be released of the duty to her Father's Gods and be inducted into the religion of her husband. And then, we talked about your duty to your bloodline. Your life is not just your own, you owe a blood debt to your many ancestors who did what was necessary to ensure that you were born.

Where Jünger improves upon this is his idea of the primeval forest. Each tree represents a man's bloodline. Some have grown tall, above the others. Some have gone off sideways and others still, have collapsed, to decompose upon the earth. These lineages grow because of the decomposition taking place in the soil. Jünger was a WARRIOR in the full sense of the word and his short work, *War as Inner Experience*, gives insight into how the warrior forms his WHY and his purpose. This is a man who grew up seeing statues and art of German heroes. He was encouraged not to just emulate their heroism but go beyond it.

There's much to learn from this forest, from our Fathers. There were lessons learned passed down to us in the form of rites, traditions, and myths. Much of this has been lost to American men. Deemed unworthy in our sophisticated "scientific" society. It must be our task to preserve what we still have and uncover what's been hidden from us. The fight for survival goes beyond you as a man. It's a struggle that's been shared by your entire bloodline.

The wars, the enemies, change. There is one constant from the beginning of mankind, however: your bloodline. This is the true struggle. This is why you must strive for superiority. I doubt many have read Frank Herbert's *God Emperor of Dune*, but in the book — which takes place a couple of thousand years after the original book — the God Emperor Leto II says he wants to teach mankind a lesson they will remember in the bones. What lesson is this? A great fear born from his prescience(vision of the future) was mankind being destroyed by a dark threat because they had failed to do what they were meant to do. Expand into the stars, into the frontier, truly diversify, and become stronger.

I too, want to teach mankind a lesson it will remember in their bones. The lesson is much the same. You can't get comfortable. You can't settle for the trad life or retvrn to some other era. You're born into this time, and you must bravely go forward. The strength of mankind, the reason we've established superiority over the whole of the earth, is our ability to master space. To master the conditions were born into and continue the fight started by the Fathers.

70.

"Life is an instinct for growth, for survival, for the accumulation of forces, for power." -Friedrich Nietzsche

The God Emperor of Dune feared some threat would stumble upon and destroy a stagnated mankind, a mankind that had refused to grow. He took charge of the species and implemented a eugenics program to prepare them for their future expanse into the unknown. He then staged an event that would force them back into the frontier. To expand further than they had ever before. We don't have a God Emperor, hell, we don't even have a Caesar, but God did give us a Nietzsche. I mentioned at the beginning this philosophy ties both Jünger and Nietzsche into one. Where Jünger forges the foundation, our why, Nietzsche provides the DIRECTION.

Nietzsche tells you what is good. The noble, the heroic, the strong, and the beautiful. This is what is loved by God. This is how you determine what is good and what is evil. Nietzsche not only distinguishes good from evil but provides the path back into nature, into the great game. From the very beginning of mankind, we have been driven toward power and growth. The worlds become more connected, and we more powerful.

We knew what the next step was. We initiated it with the SPACE RACE, but then we were pulled back to earth, dragged back into the weeds. Our instincts hidden away with pharmaceutical drugs and nefarious psychological conditioning. You cannot stop trying to grow. To accumulate power. You cannot stop fighting. The moment you do, nature will throw an apocalyptic curveball.

Nietzsche saw what must happen. You must ascend. You must go higher. To stray away from the fight for survival is to reject life in its entirety. It's the cause of all our mental illness and general malaise. You're made for this fight. To follow the Way of the Fathers. The Will to Power is instinctive, it's in the blood. It's your duty to survive into the future and prove the superiority of your bloodline.

The way the enemy wins is by separating our people from their ancestral history. Sever their Thread of Continuity and you control them. Knowing this ancestral history is vital for a people in the fight for survival. A people are better able to confront threats of the present if they have the lessons learned from their ancestors in the past. We will always be connected to the ancestors by blood, but if you aren't taught this connection, it's quite easy to become lost in the immense complexities of the world.

Severing the thread is a classic tactic of leftism. It was used to great effect by Soviet Russia and again in the United States just after World War II. Now in the modern day, you're hard-pressed to know your family history unless you take an interest in it. Your own family probably knows very little. We have no knowledge of our tribal history on top of this. Most of us are probably far removed from the tribe which puts us in the position of needing further ethnogenesis.

In previous times, you knew what you were and who your tribe was. You had a tribe, a people. Many of the European tribes merged through Manifest Destiny. We became American, but the roots were still known. And in a way, this was supposed to happen. A prerogative to renew the race.

The experience on the frontier transformed the European blood. It set us apart from our European cousins. We became differentiated, changed. The taming of the frontier was the renewal of our races, but it also changed the tribe. Americans contain strains from the many tribes that settled the New World. The power of this new race was realized in and after the Second World War. Our decline following the civil rights era is a moment of truth. Can we recover from the severing? Russia has in a way, pulled itself up, but a full recovery? Too early to tell, they're still, in a way, governed by leftism.

It's important to remember the Way of the Fathers. What made them strong and superior? You must also remember what they got wrong and make the necessary adjustments. You can still rightfully honor them while accepting they were human. You can never accept the leftist frame of being shamed by them. They were great men who helped make our country a superpower. They tamed the New World. They were the last race to be forced back into nature and conquer.

71.

Blood and soil? Or just blood?

The idea of blood and soil comes out of Germany. I enjoy how Ernst Jünger explains it in *War as Inner Experience*. His conception of blood and soil was that each man was the peak of his bloodline. Each bloodline was a growing tree in the forest. This bloodline grows from the decomposition of the people who came before. Some trees reach towering heights, others have gone sideways. Still, others have been felled.

Jünger tells us how he as a young man was raised to be a warrior. All around him were statues of German heroes he was compelled to emulate. These Germans had a keen understanding of who they were and where they came from. Something the average American doesn't have a clue about. Of what importance is the soil to a people concerned with futurism, however? I've already talked about how the soil of the New World turned the Europeans into an American. The land does change you, but ultimately, I believe you must be more attached to the blood.

I'm a futurist in my leanings. There is all this talk about how climate change is going to lead to extinction. Extinction can always happen whether by a stray meteor no one saw coming or thermonuclear war. When you think about it, mankind has all its eggs in one basket: the Earth. If we're ever to become *more*, we have to move beyond the earth. Wherever we go next will change us in the same way the frontier in the New World changed us. We don't know exactly how, but the people who take to the frontier will be changed from the people who stayed behind. The earth is truly our mother, but everything that lives will eventually die.

Blood is the most important. The soil is important to provide a foundation to launch oneself from. It can hold a nostalgic feeling in our souls, but if we are to survive and thrive, we have to move into the great unknown. The next frontier.

72.

Your duty is to the strength and future of the tribe.

We may leave the soil behind, but the blood remains. The tribe may — through ethnogenesis — become something else. But it must. Man was made to tame the frontier and through his taming of the frontier, he himself becomes changed. What did Nietzsche say about looking into the abyss? It also looks into you. We are in a position now where our people have become dispossessed by the country we founded. The country itself is actively trying to eliminate us as a threat to its sovereignty.

These times call for a return to the old ways of thinking as mastered by our ancestors. You have to find or make a new tribe. White is an identifier of your possible tribesmen. We are in the same fight for survival against the coldest of all cold monsters. Become clannish. Become brutal and ruthless. There is much to learn about the tribe and what it must become.

There is a chapter in the original *Dune*, you must read. It happens right after the Harkonnen attack on the Atreides. It deals with the side character named Thufir Hawat who is a mentat, which means a human computer — because, in this world of *Dune*, men don't trust AI. You don't get this scene in the movie; you have to read it in the book. Hawat and his wounded men have been rescued by a couple of Fremen(the native people) and this chapter in particular gives insight into how different the civilized, progressive Atreides are compared to the savage and tribal Fremen. The Fremen are a straightforward, matter of fact, hard people.

They care first and foremost about the future of the tribe. In a harsh desert world where water is the most valuable commodity, they survive by making hard decisions. A "water decision" they call it. They know and understand that everyone dies. If a man is wounded and unable to help himself, he should die so that the water in his body may be used to help the tribe survive. You see in the chapter how Hawat does everything in his power to convince the Fremen to help his wounded to safety and medical aid, but the Fremen already sees them as dead men, and the only way to help the survivors is by taking their water.

You have to begin moving away from the civilized. Begin thinking as a collective, a tribe. For the Fremen, a man's body was his own, but the water in that body belonged to the tribe. What matters is the strength and survival of the tribe. Its future supersedes any one man. We have that tribe, but we're splintered beyond recognition. There is still hope for the future.

The broken bonds and allegiances must be remade. Strengthened against the tactics of the enemy. We must become something they don't understand. We must become men of strength and savage honor. Honor is made within the tribe, not without. Nothing matters but the future of the tribe. This is how you must begin to think about the future.

73.

THE PATRICIAN ORDER

As Americans, we are twice separated from our Thread of Continuity. We lost it when our forefathers came to the New World and again, after the end of the Second World War when Americans were allowed to get plump and comfortable. The United States, like all countries since based its founding on that of Ancient Rome. One more lesson we can take from the Romans is to form our own PATRICIAN ORDER in the spirit of the Way of the Fathers. The Patricians were seen as the ruling families of Rome. From where did the Patricians originate? When Romulus founded Rome, the first 100 men appointed as senators were called the Fathers and their descendants became the Patrician class.

Religion for the early Romans was decentralized into domestic cults. Each family had its own religion and its own Gods. Ancestor worship was also extremely important to the Romans. Contrast this with modern Americans who almost have no religion, no God, and no knowledge of their familial heritage. This lack of familial knowledge must change and the way to change it is by re-establishing the Patricians. It starts with you and recognizing your charge as a man. A new Patrician Order must be formed to bring salvation to the American race.

What does it mean to be a Patrician? It means you are a steward of a bloodline that extends back to the beginning of mankind and while you breathe, you're charged with keeping that bloodline going. It's your responsibility to have children. It's your responsibility to teach your sons the Way of the Fathers and ensure they carry on the fight after you die. At its core, it's once again becoming responsible for yourself, and not just for yourself, but for your family and bloodline. Now you can't be a senator like the first Fathers of Rome, but you can etch your name as one of the Americans Fathers that leads the race to salvation. It's to be your mission to link up with other Patricians, take blood oaths, and form brotherhoods for the good of the race and to grow the power of your family.

The Roman Patricians were more than just senators of Rome. They were the high priests of their family's domestic religion. They performed all the religious rites and kept their hearth fires burning. Now, they weren't just priests, they were also warriors who — unlike our modern, disgusting politicians — fought for Rome. Many died in service to Rome in its wars. Think less of the priestly aspect of being a Patrician as you are now a part of a WARRIOR RELIGION and your religious rites are those of strength, survival, and fighting. Later on, I will touch on what it will take to be a modern Hoplite or Legionnaire. It is the American way to be responsible for yourself and we must return to our stern old traditions.

Make yourself proud of the name and bloodline your father gave you. Do your diligence to learn as much as you can about your heritage, look for heroism in your bloodline that you can both be proud of and pass on to your children. Worship your ancestors. Teach your children to do the same. If you can't find anything, then it starts with you. Do things that will make you remembered by your descendants. This is something you should be striving for already. When the time comes it will be the might of the Patricians, the American Fathers, that guide our people out of hell. Who get us back on the path of Manifest Destiny and light the fire of Holy War.

A Patrician is charged with the stewardship of his bloodline. He will keep or create new stern traditions to keep his family safe from the psychological warfare waged by our hostile government. Being responsible for himself and his family, he no longer relies on the government or "dem programs." He's to make himself a warrior to show his devotion to God and pass on this knowledge to his descendants. He is to HONOR his ancestors and do his part to bring glory to his family name. A Patrician must do his part to forge blood-alliances with fellow Americans. He must keep his friends and judge his enemies. This is what it means to be a Father with a capital F.

The Way of the Fathers is the stern old traditions of our ancestors, the keeping of the Sacred Fire, and the creation of the new Patrician Order to both create and protect a new Thread of Continuity.

74.

A religion like Christianity is universalistic. Anyone can be Christian so long as they accept Jesus Christ as their savior. Now it's entirely possible that our ancestors looked at Christianity differently from our contemporaries. As in, yes, this man is a Christian, but he's not my people. This universalist form allowed the religion to effectively conquer the world and the new religion, which has taken its place, has effectively kept its morality. The enemy wears the religion like a skinsuit to mask its anti-White hatred. It's hatred for you. There are few real Christians left.

Our people have felt the spiritual void left by its absence. This religion greatly inspired thumos and true religious feeling in our ancestors, but what our parents and grandparents underestimated was the capability of our enemy to subvert society. They have severed the Thread of Continuity between us and those who came before us. We don't understand the religious or world feeling of our ancestors. We don't buy into what they bought into. Neopagans have tried to fill the void left by Christianity and while they may understand the world feeling of our ancestors, they will not be able to duplicate the religious feeling. There's much strife between the few Christians left and the even smaller minority of Neopagans, strife better spent against our enemies than each other. We hold more in common than different. The door is wide open for a new religious feeling — Christian or Pagan.

What must be understood is religion is much more than what Gods you pray to. Oswald Spengler believed religion to be existence itself. It encompassed everything from religious rites, culture, customs, traditions, art, and even math. How you live is your religion. Christian or Pagan, you are American. You're a part of the Aryan inheritance which all Americans and Europeans trace back to before the Ancient Greeks and Romans. You had ancestors who were Pagan, as well as Christian. We must honor them both. We cannot restore the Thread of Continuity, but we can forge new thread, and honor our blood the way we were meant to.

It's important to understand, that in our known history, there hasn't been a return to any prior religious feelings. You cannot go back. You cannot RETVRN. The only way out is through. You can only go forward. Once the thread has been severed, a new path must be forged. This is what I mean by the door being wide open.

The new RELIGIOUS FEELING will emerge only after its disciples have strung together victories against our enemies. With that in mind, you have to adopt Spengler's definition of religion and devote yourself to a WARRIOR RELIGION. Understand that the foundation to any people is the brotherhood of armed men. Friedrich Nietzsche himself rightly observed that the FREE MAN is a warrior. You can only be free if you're willing to be responsible for yourself and prepared to sacrifice yourself and others to maintain that freedom. This is the first step any new religious feeling or Warrior Religion must take. Make yourself a warrior and make friends who are also warriors. Swear blood oaths to each other.

It must be noted that the strongest bonds — outside of family — are the bonds between people of the same race. Pierre van den Berghe did a series of studies in Africa that proved that ethnicity is the driver of a people. That said, as I've written earlier in this book(in fact, at the very beginning), it's important to forge bonds with Americans who are defined as White people with lineages stretching back to before the War Between the States. It's possible to take in people who do not match this description, but they should be men of race who choose to abandon their prior ethnicity, in order to be American. If they're not willing to do this, they should not be accepted, for when the chips are down, men always retreat to their ethnic strongholds. I'm not saying you can't be friends with them, but don't trust them with your life.

The current power structure is indeed designed precisely to break the bonds between Americans. Propaganda taught to us in school push things like "race only being skin deep," "America is an idea," "everybody can be American" we will succeed in this country based on merit, and Whites should be especially ashamed of their heritage of slavery and racism. These talking points are all designed to isolate Americans from each other to allow very bad people to acquire more power and wealth, at our expense. It's not an understatement to say we're entering a war our ancestors lost before we were even born. But you must never give up. Never, never surrender. As Ennius said, "The victor is not victorious if the vanquished does not consider himself so." This was the mentality that made the Romans — our spiritual ancestors — the greatest empire to walk the earth.

Yes, civil rights are designed to take away opportunities from Americans and give them to foreigners. Yes, your opportunities are quickly drying up thanks to the seemingly endless immigration into the United States that our "leaders" turn a blind eye to. Yes, other races can practice nepotism and racism, at our expense, while if the government catches you doing the same, they will persecute you over them. Again, yes, the other races do this. They segregate, prefer their own, and take care of their own. The power structure works overtime to "marginalize(to borrow one of their words)" the American. It's best seen in the current day by the assault on the 2nd Amendment by highlighting ONLY the instances where a White Man shoots some poor black saint.

Yes, all these things are working against us. But you must fight. That means taking care of your own. Preferring your own. You just need to be more discreet than a corporation's human resources department. While our chips are down, you must aim to stay under the radar. Remember who the real enemy is. The blacks, foreigners, don't matter. Had this country been run the way it was supposed to, it would have been rolled over and crushed a long time ago.

Against all odds, we will prevail. If you do not believe me, just look back at human history and remember what Jonathan Bowden had to say about the matter: "98% of all history of any importance was accomplished by dead White European males." It's in our blood.

75.

I want to speak to the character of our new people. We must HONOR our ancestors, near and far. All Western peoples' point of origin is Ancient Greece and Rome. We share this spiritual heritage with all the European tribes, English, German, French, etc. We can know and understand those who are like us, whereas an African or Chinese will not understand our values. That said, Americans are a NEW tribe, a combination of all the Europeans forced back into nature in the New World and forged anew. Our near history changed our values in a way only an American understands in his blood.

Americans have a more visceral and raw understanding of nature, of might is right. Our ancestors were forced, damn near unprepared, back into nature. All the comforts of civilization gone. Our ancestors had settlements that suffered heavy casualties or died out entirely. They were shipped into a world they didn't know or understand — and through their strong religious feeling, they kept fighting. They found a way to survive and thrive. Near the end of the Great War when the Americans entered the fight, Europeans were impressed both with the size of the American man and the superiority of their equipment. Our ancestors made themselves hard, manly, and industrious.

The country we live in today was founded by warlike and vigilant men driven by the frontier spirit. Men who defeated the strongest empire in the world at the time and then, went on to tame the frontier. We must always admire and revere this but recognize that not everything they did was good. The country they founded was subverted as early as the 1930s with the emergence of communism and arguments can be made that it was as early as the Civil War. Some things were vitally important to tribes of men that our ancestors disregarded, and we pay the price for it today. The republic they made did not last. Freedom of the press allowed men to take the reins of this republic. It resembles more an oligarchy than anything else today.

The press — which was so respected during the beginning of the country — became a joke. They're a tool of our enemies to swindle us from all power. A new president every four years means America is a terrible country to be allied with. We're untrustworthy because the actions or alliances of one president can be undone by the next. Our courts have been gamed by our enemies to bring in such policies like civil rights which effectively undermines the United States constitution. Our politicians today try to convince you that America isn't even a country, it's an idea and anyone can be an American. You must ignore this and discriminate ruthlessly.

Not talked about enough is the reality that the creation of the United States was the creation of a new people. It wasn't just a country or a state or an idea. It was made for specific tribes that came together on the frontier through ethnogenesis. This happens to all peoples over time, we just happen to be the last to undergo this process. As such, we must hold sacred the properties and values of our race, that our European cousins might not necessarily understand, while also making adjustments to what didn't work for our forefathers. American history taught in schools spends a lot of time talking about the institutions established in Washington, but not what made us a people: the frontier.

It cannot be understated how much VITALITY the frontier gave the American race. Our birth rates were off the charts in times when childhood death was common, there were no hospitals or any of the technology we have today. Our women were having ten to twelve children. Absolutely insane when compared to the latest numbers that have White women barely doing replacement numbers. Our men had to learn how to be responsible for themselves. They had to know how to hunt, farm, and fight off Indian raids. Many built their own houses, had their businesses, were frontiersmen, tradesmen, and more.

The frontier provided this. We were a people trying to do as all people do: survive and thrive in nature. We had seemingly boundless wilderness before us. Our ancestors were taken into the spirit we call MANIFEST DESTINY. We believed the New World was ours for the taking and we fought our way from sea to shining sea. Our enemies want to highlight the seeming "evil" of our ancestors for doing this without highlighting how brutal the Indians we faced were. This yearning for the frontier, for Manifest Destiny, is something biological, primordial even. It was right in every way and our Great Work is expanding into the next frontier. To revive our race's vitality.

You can say what you will about the religious texts left to us. Maybe they're the words of The Gods or not. But if you want to know what it is God wants from you, you need only examine human history. Natural law is the way of God. God selects for the strong, Christian, or Pagan. The strong impose their will on the world and God created America to train the faithful.

With that in mind, the most important trait established by our forefathers is the 2nd Amendment. A paper Constitution isn't enough. Weapons must be part of our living constitution, a part of our religion. It's cliché to talk about how the right to bear arms fends off tyranny, but it's absolutely true. There is no other reason why our enemies go after the 2nd Amendment with all their zeal, doing everything in their power to chip away at it. It must become more than an amendment. Bearing arms kept our ancestors alive on the wild frontier.

There can never be any law or policy that disrupts our ability to defend ourselves from any and everything, including our own military. Any person pushing this ideology, no matter how innocent it may seem, is trying to destroy the American race.

76.

Leftists can't comprehend WHY the American founders implemented the 2nd Amendment. They have this fantastical belief that if the founding fathers could see an AR-15, they would have had second thoughts about the 2nd Amendment. This is with the full knowledge that the colonies had just finished liberating themselves from the strongest empire in the world. If you look at history and the traditions of our ancestors, you can only conclude that the American founders didn't go far enough. The right to bear arms shouldn't be some amendment to a paper constitution. It shouldn't be something that could be changed or infringed upon in any way. The ones that try, show themselves to be un-American at best and out to destroy Americans at worst.

Weapons should be considered a part of our religion. A racial birthright. All our ancestors understood this to be true. When you read a book like Coulanges' *The Ancient City*, you see just how important FIRE — which we take for granted today — was to the first men. They treated the hearth fire like a God and the center of their domestic religions. The first men mastered fire and fire gave them an unfair advantage over nature. So unfair an advantage, primitive men believed it a sacrilege against nature and The Gods. Fire took mankind to the top of the food chain. The primary weapons of war today are FIREARMS.

Fire is still as vital today as it was to our ancestors. Another way of thinking about fire is as energy. If you review human history, what you find is the countries and peoples who unleashed the most energy or FIRE won the wars. The North over the South in the War between the States, both World Wars, are examples of this. You can even include wars that we consider lost, like Vietnam or Afghanistan. We didn't really lose those wars as our retreat did not lead to foreigners claiming America for themselves. Fire is an absolute necessity for sovereignty.

Religion requires ACTION for it to become alive. For it to even exist. If you cannot take action because you don't have fire or energy, your religion is dead in the water. Long before we had firearms, fire and energy were winning wars. Ancient peoples used fire to burn enemy supplies or strongholds. Even before it was used offensively, it provided warmth to those who sat around it, revitalized the energy of those who took shelter by it. It was an unfair advantage. The attack on the 2nd Amendment and by extension, fire, is a grievous and unforgivable attack on our ability to exist. To be sovereign.

The 2nd Amendment is primordial to mankind, a virtue of survival, and deserves more than to be just a piece of paper debated upon by bad actors. There should be no debates. Weapons are part of our religion, our embodied law. To lose this is tantamount to committing suicide. Never give your enemies the time of day on this. Any who go after it, regardless of the angle, are enemies of our people and our religion. Part of our birthright as men is gaining mastery over fire and it should never be infringed upon.

77.

My recommendations are as follows:

Every American man should be armed. The brotherhood of armed men is the foundation of a people. Furthermore, he should be trained to be a warrior. I would not be opposed to every American man being made to serve in the military. Weapons evolve and Americans must be able to keep up with the technology of the times.

The race must become extremely clannish and tough. We have seen what happens when our nepotism is criminalized and foreigners, who only entered the country yesterday, can practice without fear of persecution. What we have before us is a country that's been taken from its rightful heirs. To win it back will require clannish toughness.

The brotherhood of armed men is the franchise. All power is with them. Any rights of the franchise should not be given to women or foreigners. Women act on their feelings for safety and acceptance and have shown that they cannot be depended on to make the hard decisions. Foreigners, obviously, have the interests of their own race in mind.

The frontier is before us. Our own country has been taken and it must be reconquered, but efforts must be made afterwards to steer the wheel of mankind forward. To take us where we haven't before. To discover new frontiers.

78.

What should be the religious rites of a new AMERICAN Warrior Religion?

Blood is of the highest importance. A man must prove his lineage was in the New World before the Civil War to be a part of the race. A society gets created by blood. There has never been a multiethnic empire. Our ancestors have been Pagans, they have been Christians. Our own time is marked by the void of religious feeling. Most believe there is some higher power or that there is no God.

A Warrior Religion should believe that God himself is unknown to us, for our people have moved too far from His Golden Path. We won't truly know God again until we get back on the Golden Path. We can, however, make some assumptions about the nature of God. Human history shows us he selects for the strong, those who win at any cost. Our God is a War God, as such, you can assume that the sacrifice of blood is important to this deity. Perhaps, we should do as the Scythians did and cut off the right arms of our enemies as sacrifice to this God. Always remember that nature is savage and eternal.

Now life is more than war, but we must realize as said in the Book of Job that "life upon this earth is warfare." War calls us back to life, but it's a double-edged sword. While it can revitalize the race, it can also destroy it. This makes it of vital importance to be masters of war, and to excel above all others. Virtu — martial excellence — must be encouraged in all our men and encouraged to the extreme. Everything must be done to light the fire in men's souls.

Speaking of fire, fire is sacred and primordial to mankind. All early societies have a story about the discovery of fire. The most known is the Greek tale of Prometheus stealing fire from Zeus to give to man. It was seen as a crime for which he was eternally punished. The Greeks and Romans held fire as sacred. Before and after the emergence of their pantheons we remember today, they all had domestic religions. Each family had their own deities, and they all worshipped the hearth fire as a God.

Families would make sure to have a meal next to this fire, careful to leave an extra plate of food for their dead ancestors who they believed walked their lands in death. We still share meals together as families today if you ever wondered where the practice originated. It's not hard to see how fire became so important to our ancestors. Imagine a primitive man trying to survive in the wilderness, building a fire, a fire his father had taught him to make. Long after the father had passed, he was still keeping his son safe and warm.

Fire itself is more than even this. It's also a weapon that helped mankind rise to the top of the food chain. Fire is still used in weapons. Your gun uses fire, more reason why weapons must be a part of a Warrior Religion. Fire and blood appear to be the pinnacles of man's dominance over other species and peoples in nature. Fire must be made sacred again. Pay tribute to this force which could have only been given to man by some God, perhaps our War God.

Our ancestors accomplished much through traditions and rites passed from one generation to the next. This Way of the Fathers must be reinstated. Instinct is more valuable than any other force in the universe. It's the reason we've lasted as long as we have. Instinct cannot be disregarded in favor of some "expert's" opinion. Almost all cultures favored the virgin for marriage. Do you want to know why? Science discovered that the FIRST man a woman sleeps with implants his genes on her eggs and her offspring, regardless of who is the father is at the time of conception.

The continuation of the race and species is of concern to a Warrior Religion. As long as we just remain on the earth, we have all our eggs sitting in one basket, waiting for the death of the solar system or a random strike from a meteor. We must strive to move into the great beyond.

This continuation of race expands to the individual level. If you're alive today, your bloodline stretches back to the beginning of mankind. This is very special and must be honored. You owe a duty to the blood to leave behind children to carry on your bloodline.

79.

Tame the Wilderness

Americans have a reputation. That reputation as of late has been tainted by the decadence and sloth of our parents, grandparents, and even ourselves. Our government's mission is to spread the rainbow flag across the globe. To bring the gays to the deserts of the middle east and the browns to Europe and America. But our reputation wasn't always so. Our ancestors were dropped off in the New World with almost nothing. In addition to their battle with nature, they were forced into a racial Holy War with the Indians.

Some of the first settlements didn't make it. Others suffered heavy casualties, losing as much as half their populations in their fight for survival. Our ancestors were forced back into nature. The last people to be so — and they were transformed by the experience. They became something different from our European counterparts. They held their ground, eventually defeating the British Empire to gain their independence. They did so with a ragged army that couldn't even provide shoes to all its soldiers. They found a way.

The new American then had to secure their country and their borders, they were thrust further into the frontier, into open conflict with the Indians. There are many reasons Americans were taken by the spirit of Manifest Destiny. It was the natural pecking order in action. The American competed with the English, the French, and the natives for positioning and territory. You saw on the frontier barbarism not seen for hundreds of years. But within a century, from the founding of the country, our ancestors reached the Pacific Coast of California. The frontier itself was closed in 1890.

In under a hundred and twenty years, our ancestors conquered a vast continent comparable to the size of Russia, China, or India. This is the American race quality. We have it in us to tame the wilderness, to conquer steppes, and frontiers. But that race quality isn't something that's granted to you by the nature of being American. You have to strive for it. Strive for superiority. Be better than your competition. Be the best. ARISTEIA — noble excellence — is what the Ancient Greks called it.

This country isn't yours anymore. It's been taken by our enemies. Do you understand what this means? You are back on the frontier, almost in the same position as your ancestors. You have almost nothing, the constitution of your ancestors has already been subverted. They're just slowly chipping away at whatever power the American still has and they will keep going slowly because WHY will you move against the next minor infraction when you've already accepted the previous hundred minor infractions? You must be wise to their way of warfare and pioneer a superior way.

The situation the American faces today seems bleak. It seems like he is in a worse position than his ancestors on the frontier. But this is just a mirage. It's the same condition, the same fight for survival. Yes, the country is "settled." Yes, the enemy is using the government of our forefathers against us. But the fight for survival wages on, only the methods required must be more cerebral. You must enter the shadows, enter the underworld itself.

The enemy can unleash overwhelming force, this is true, which makes it imperative that you fly under the radar. That you don't get caught in fed operations like protests. Protests are a weapon of the enemy and only the enemy can protest. There is no reason for you to be at events like this. Your way must be the mastering this new frontier. Finding or making paths around or through the enemy's bulwarks. Building a foundation from which your sons can carry on this war because make no mistake, there is no end in sight.

How much ground has been surrendered by our parents and grandparents? How much strength as a people have we lost? How much racial cohesion? There is much ground that must be made up to even give Americans a chance and that's fine. Our ancestors were wholly unprepared for the New World when they first arrived. They adapted. They overcame.

Where you are now is where you must build from. Everywhere around you is the frontier. The regime you live under is hostile. The foreigners have a deranged racial hatred against you. You have to navigate the wilderness. Master it. Tame it.

There are no blueprints for this. You live in a massive country with over three hundred million inhabitants. Everyone's situation will be different. Some better off than others. If it's in your ability, maybe look for enclaves of your people to form bastions of strength within the empire. The goal, however, is to prove your superiority, prove your worth, find ways to succeed no matter where you are. You can't give in to the despair of not having a cookie-cutter way out of hell. Academia tries to scam Americans into believing something like this.

Your way becomes whatever gets you ahead. Whatever makes you superior. Whatever keeps you in the shadows, out of the sight of your enemies. This effort goes beyond all of us. You must prepare your children to carry on this fight. To understand what's been taken from them and prepare them as best as you can to take it back. Everything is on the table.

Your path to taming the wilderness starts with you. Making yourself a FATHER of the new American race. Doing what you can to be the best. To lay the foundation for your descendants to carry on the fight, to induct them into a Warrior Religion, and take oaths to win this bloody religious war. It must be ingrained into our people to win the Holy War, to spread like an unquenchable fire until our people are rightfully back on top. The final frontier is waiting.

80.

Devotion.

Devotion is a word you don't hear often in our culture. There's an inherent revulsion to it on the part of our enemies who promote everything but devotion. In a Warrior Religion, DEVOTION should be a sacred word. But it's more than a word to disciples, it's a mindset. An aesthetic to aim for. How do you show your devotion to God and a Warrior Religion? By doing your part to move your people to the Golden Path.

Training both physically for war and health is devotion. You must treat training as RITUS(Latin for Ritual Action). As a man, you are made for war. It's shameful to let your body fall to such a state that you cannot fight. Be the example for both your children and your people. Make yourself the opposite of the degenerate slop that makes up the ranks of our enemies. Likewise, spend the proper time honing your craft.

Be devoted to keeping the Sacred Fire of your ancestors lit and adhere to The Way of the Fathers. Your bloodline stretches back to the beginning of mankind. If you have children, make sure they understand the importance of this. Know about your heritage and family history. Maintain the rites and traditions you know, create new ones if they are lost. We cannot let the Thread of Continuity be severed again.

Be devoted to Aristeia. Noble excellence. It's easy to check out of the modern world, especially in America, where they're looking for every opportunity to shut the door on our people. You must be devoted to being better, superior to the point where they can't ignore you. Keep your hands on as much power as possible.

Be devoted to God. God may be unknown to us, but we know that if we strive for the Golden Path and live in adherence to nature, we will find our way to God again. Ask him for the strength and courage to do what's necessary.

Extreme devotion leads to religious ecstasy, which is better known as FANATICISM. This is your goal.

81.

God created America to train the faithful.

It takes a particular type of man to make it in the New World. The next test is coming.

82.

There is a deep gulf between the Warrior and the Soldier in the modern world. There are points where the two overlap, but one must understand that the Soldier came about only after the emergence of democratic warfare. It's beyond the scope of this work to get into the weeds about the differences between the two. For the most part, only a Soldier can be a Warrior in the modern day, but not all Soldiers are Warriors. The ways of war have been monopolized by the state. This is something a Warrior Religion should be devoted to changing, but until real power can be wrestled from the coldest of all cold monsters, you must cultivate the prowess of a Warrior as an underdog and guerrilla.

Oftentimes, it's easy to get caught up in the romance of what you want war to be. We lament the advancements of technology that wrench the importance of skill and excellence from the Warrior who still strives mightily to be the best, but unlike the Grek Hoplite, who understood that skill and martial excellence made up say 80% of his chances for survival and glory, the modern Warrior's devotion to his craft may account for only 20%. Fortuna, luck, chance, holds the majority sway over the Warrior's fate in our time. Technology has made war into a meat grinder. A Warrior can be picked off by a gunship high in the sky long before he gets a chance to raise his rifle in defense. This is a reality of the world we've been born into, but it doesn't take away from the necessity of the task. Mankind will always need Warriors.

The Solider is a professional. He's paid to fight. In some ways, he's been separated from the spiritual and intellectual aspects of being a Warrior. Our academic caste enjoys poking fun at the Soldier as being a brute. Now this is slander as the military does value education. The scholarly intellectual is perhaps, missing more of the equation than the Soldier that refuses "higher education."

A divide between the Soldier and the Warrior that must be dissolved is the spiritual view of warfare which you don't see in Western men as much as you saw in say, eastern samurai. The closest you get to the eastern Warrior spirituality would be the German Stormtrooper Ernst Jünger. His book, *War as Inner Experience*, is his most underrated work which deals specifically with the spiritual in war. He saw the Warrior as manly and noble in the war where the spirit of the Warrior met the storm of steel and technology in the most brutal meat grinder the world has ever seen. Most of the horrific views of war we have today originate with The Great War that Jünger came out of. You can list all the medals awarded to Jünger, but I believe the biggest testament to his power was the fact that he was wounded fourteen times between 1914 and 1918. He kept coming back for more, never stopping until the war ended. Until his country backed down. That is the spirit of the Western Warrior.

Something to consider when you analyze Ernst Jünger's spirituality toward warfare: he became Catholic before he died, but if you read *War as Inner Experience*, you realize that the Jünger was not Christian in any sense, and at the same time, he was perhaps more spiritual than any religion at the time claimed to be. He believed in God, though his God seemed to be — rightfully — a War God like MARS. Jünger believed in blood and soil as well as ancestor worship. You are part of a bloodline rising out of the ground like a tree in an ancient forest, feeding off the soil and decomposition of the men who came before you. He very much held primordial belief structures about the world.

The Warrior is more than his prowess in battle, though it is that prowess that will define him. His intellect, his spirituality made him more of what he is. It's what separates him from the professional. You see so much psychological damage in our Soldiers after they have finished their military commitments and I truly believe it's because they weren't brought up to be Warriors. Our men are oriented toward the pursuit of "progress," liberal democracy, and the intellect. What's most ironic about the latter is this intellectual pursuit leaves out the reality of nature and what it means to a man. It makes our men unprepared for the war they fight on behalf of us all.

Men are hardwired to be Warriors. It's what we are meant to be, made by God to be, but men in our time are raised to reject this birthright. To believe testosterone bad, that our innate nature is evil. It's no wonder when our Soldiers return home, they find themselves broken. They were used and abused by our government. It is a great crime against our people, and we will have retribution.

83.

Belief structures win wars. By default, we're raised into a leftist belief structure. Most men get taught that manliness is toxic. They must fear it taking control of them. They're taught to believe in equality and equity. The world isn't fair so we must try to make it fair. You have to believe in progress. The world isn't perfect, but you have to try to make it so.

These men, despite their upbringing, get called upon to serve their homeland which invades some third-world country to bring liberal democracy and lgbt rights to foreigners. The military does its job in preparing these men for what must they do, but there's a disconnect in the training and sociological upbringing that leaves these men psychologically damaged afterward. The argument while it was happening during the "Global War on Terror" was that it always existed, and it went diagnosed. Maybe this is true, but I have a different explanation. These men had no understanding of the way of the world. Their experiences fighting for the US military brought them up to speed on a level they couldn't handle. They were not prepared for what they were forced to experience.

Our people are raised to believe in a fantasy world that doesn't exist. It takes time to process the lies and deceit. Men raised to understand the world as it is, would not be psychologically damaged in the same way. Our people raised in these fantasy belief structures become victims of the cruel masters running the show. Psychological casualties. Not just our Soldiers and Warriors, but all who are brought up under the empire. When you see the real way of the world, you can't help to see the cruel joke being played out in what's supposed to be the greatest country in the world.

84.

When your worldview meets the Desolation of the Real

There is scene in old movie, *The Matrix*, when the freedom fighter Morpheus shows his new recruit, Neo, what the real world looks like after revealing he's been living in a computer simulation his entire life. The real world is a barren, unlivable wasteland where mankind must live underground to survive and avoid detection by machines. This is a good, memorable scene that many people have seen, and you must keep it in mind when I talk about sensitive subject: post-traumatic stress syndrome(PTSD). PTSD became an important issue during the Global War on Terror in the early 2000s. I was a freshman in high school when the war started and remember watching the news with anticipation while it was going on. I was certain I would enlist when I graduated. Four years later, however, I did not enlist and it's a decision I both regret and don't regret at the same time.

Why didn't I enlist? As a sensitive young man, it dawned on me that the Afghanis were never really a threat to the United States. The military domination of the Afghanis was total(though the United States was never able to spiritually defeat them), Afghanistan never stood a chance. It was like a bully picking on a little kid. There was no chance of an Afghani invasion of US soil. What would I be doing? I'd be risking my legs getting blown off for some police action half a world away. I wouldn't be protecting my country. Around this time too, we started hearing about PTSD. How it was being properly diagnosed now vs how soldiers with PTSD were wrongly branded as cowards and executed for it during The Great War.

Now the experts made the argument that PTSD was going to happen to our soldiers. It was unavoidable. So, joining the military, in a way, meant you were signing up to get your legs blown off by an enemy that was no threat to your people and your mind was going to get fucked up. I made the decision not to enlist. I both regret and don't regret the decision as I believe every man has the duty to become a warrior, but I also wasn't interested in dying in a seemingly meaningless police action. The expert analysis of PTSD always seemed off to me and as I began my real education(you can't trust the education you receive from the state), I realized the reason why so many American soldiers were getting PTSD in the "War on Terror." It all comes back to *The Matrix* scene I described above.

Americans are raised into the ideology of "liberal democracy." They're taught a specific worldview — by worldview, I mean a specific way of looking at the world. For example, Americans are taught to believe that liberal democracy is the greatest form of government on the earth, and it's been perfected by the American experiment. That violence is bad and only committed by bigoted people. That with democracy, you get the most peaceful and profitable form of government. In a democracy, everyone is equal. You don't the type of thing you saw in Nazi Germany where the Germans persecuted what they saw as the inferior people, the Jews. We're very conscious of making sure everyone is equal, especially after our troubled history where our ancestors owned slaves.

America is a country where anyone can come here and "pick themselves up by their bootstraps." If you work hard enough, you will succeed. And we are filled with this special mission to spread liberal democracy across the planet. To give everyone the same chances we have. When the War on Terror kicked off, for example, we got stories about how the Afghanis treated their women. How they cut off people's heads live on the internet. That oppressed people were living there, held down by terrorists and a corrupt regime. We went to Afghanistan to end terrorists and bring women's studies to their schools.

Why then, under such noble cause, did we have so many soldiers return home with PTSD? Why did the war start fucking with their minds? These men were raised under the worldview of liberal democracy and when they went to fight in the Global War on Terror, they were met with the DESOLATION of the real world. I've often talked about how most Americans believe they're living in a fantasy world. It doesn't exist anywhere except in America at certain times. These men were confronted with a world that completely disrupted the way they thought the world worked. When met with the most extreme trauma a man can experience(war) and that the way you thought the world worked was not at all how the world worked created the rise in PTSD that we saw in the War on Terror.

It's very much akin to *The Matrix* analogy of someone not being ready to be "unplugged." Being forced to adapt to the real world in the most extreme of environments is too much for many to do. Especially in young men who have lived relatively comfortable lives compared to the people they were fighting halfway across the world. They were also forced to realize things like RACE and TRIBE matter when they're trying to win the "hearts and minds" of the people there. The cultural differences between American and Afghani were night and day. Americans are not taught the way the world is, but rather how liberal experts believe the world should be. This resulted in terrible psychological damage to our fighting men.

Progress is another big value taught to Americans. We must always be progressing. Our worldview is what we think the world should be, not what it is. It doesn't cross the minds of our impressionable youth that the world is a completely different animal and when the cards turn against the United States, Americans WILL revert to the true way of the world. You must fight against the American desire to say, "Well, it shouldn't be like that, we need to try to make it better." You can't. Nature will humble you every time.

What happened to our fighting men is evidence of the gross incompetence and malevolence of our ruling class. A man raised to understand the world as it is with all the brutality it entails will be better prepared to deal with the extreme situations soldiers encounter in the Middle East. Our people would be better prepared to do what's necessary in war, rather than forcing our soldiers into ridiculous rules of engagement. A people that cannot cope with reality, that has allowed itself to grow soft and lose its edge, become a people on the chopping block of nature. The moment you think you've mastered nature, that she no longer applies to you, is the moment nature sows the seeds of your destruction. Rather, you have to raise your sons to know the true way of the world. The absolute brutality and cruelty they may see, experience, or may even be forced to commit in service to their people. That sometimes "Survival itself sometimes involved savage decisions," as said by the author Frank Herbert.

The world ain't all sunshine and rainbows. We must prepare our people for all it entails if we care about surviving and thriving in it. You do a disservice to yield your sons and daughters from the way of the world.

85.

The Warrior's Belief Structure

The first step in creating a Warrior's Belief Structure is to understand how the world works. The natural order of things. Our "experts" make many claims about the supposed superiority of the scientific method. What you will find oftentimes is that science almost never disagrees with the powers that be and the press whom they speak through. They will have you believe your leaders are the biggest proponents of science and expertise. They do their job so well that to talk about what I'm about to talk about before the uninitiated is akin to committing seppuku. Most aren't willing to tolerate anything that disagrees with the common sentiment.

How does the world work? Natural law boils down to three words: Might is Right. You can find a book by the same name that does a brilliant job of helping man to understand the doctrines of nature. You've likely heard in your public education the expression, "History is written by the victors." Not only do the victors write their own history, by their MIGHT, they determine our values. When you're the strongest, what you say becomes the truth. Your values get imposed upon your subjects.

Now, how do you go about becoming the strongest? Contrary to what you hear in school, our ancestors are the best resources in this subject. They became the best and passed down their lessons learned as rites and traditions. Those rites and traditions became "disproven" when tyrants took control and sought to pull out all the stops to hold onto their power. One man is easy to deal with. Easy to silence. This is as true today as it was in the past. One man could be conquered by many, regardless of how strong he was. The numbers would eventually overwhelm.

The brotherhood of armed men is the foundation of a people. In almost every European tribe, a military brotherhood became the foundation of the whole. Men were raised to serve under a lord. When they became overpopulated, the young were sent out in war bands to terrorize their neighbors and make their own marks on the world. As much as our regime likes to talk about equality, there is a distinct difference in physical prowess between men and women. Men are born to fight. There is a reason why women's rights took off when it did. It forced men to include women in activities that were once male-only and prevented men from acting as they normally would or organizing in a way perilous to the empire.

The military brotherhoods were almost always men of the same race. Race is more than skin color. People of the same race trust each other more than they would trust an outsider. Jeff Bezos after acquiring Whole Foods paid for studies on how he could reduce the chances of his workers going on strike. Do you know what these studies found?

Whole Foods stores that were more DIVERSE were less likely to organize and strike. Stores with the lowest diversity were more likely to strike. Do you see now why every corporation likes to talk about diversity being "our strength?" In reality, it's their strength. We live in a comfortable world, seemingly separated from the savagery of nature, but if you look to somewhere that hasn't been neutered, say a prison, what do you see? The inmates all organize into gangs that are segregated by RACE. Ethnicity is the driver of a people. It's how we survived and how we will continue to survive.

This isn't a matter of learning to hate different races. The empire tries to frame it this way to sow discord and stifle rebellion. An ethnically diverse society will be at war with itself. Multiethnic societies will always be ruled by ethnic grievances. I don't believe you have to always like people of the same race, that you won't fall into similar disputes as you would with people of different races, but in general, you will form stronger bonds with people of the same race. Hell, you can have all the diverse friends you want, but when the chips are down, everyone retreats back to their own race to make their stand.

You make your mark on the world through the tribe and race. Every successful empire did this. There has never been a successful multiethnic empire. Now empires may employ different tribes to help them in battles. The Romans with the Germans, for example. You must remember, however, they worked together but they weren't integrated. Germanic tribes were often used by Romans as Calvary — they weren't put into the legions.

If you have doubts about anything I've said, let's look back at the greatness of America. Everything great this country has done was accomplished before the push for diversity in the 1960-70s. Victory in the World Wars, becoming an economic powerhouse, and the moon landing all took place before diversity. They were accomplished when the country was 90% White. One thing to remember is that founding stock Americans didn't refer to themselves as White. That is a recent phenomenon. They referred to themselves as American and Anglo-Saxon.

Settlers on the frontier were often forced to join militias to protect their territories from Indians. You can see these groups as war bands. Every boy was raised to be capable with a rifle and fight when necessary. He was taught to make fire and how to survive in the wilderness. We didn't have the pretenses of being kind and harmless. The push across the frontier made our people hard. People had to be responsible for themselves. There was no welfare, no police to call on when you had an emergency.

There were no cars or planes or even paved roads on the frontier. You were on foot or horseback. There are records of the men who weighed on average 140-150lbs being able to deadlift triple their body weight as on average. Americans were built tough. The dangers of the frontier made them clannish, and they were ruthless in their pursuit of Manifest Destiny. There were no fantasies about what it took to make it in nature.

Men raised to know exactly what it takes to survive in nature are not going to have the same psychological damage as those ruthlessly forced into reality by our government. That they, along with their ancestors who came before them, are in the same fight for survival. Did you know almost every people had a form of ancestor worship in their history? What your educators fail to tell you is that you are part of a bloodline that goes back to the beginning of mankind. That's something special that needs to be protected. You owe a duty to your blood and as long as you're alive, you are the steward of that bloodline. You are not just an individual, you are a part of a bloodline and a race. You have to work with your kin in order to secure your people's future.

This is how you find the STRENGTH to be what you're meant to be. To do what must be done in nature. To be a warrior is a great honor. It's something you crave in the blood, on a biological level. To bring glory to your bloodline and people. I'm willing to bet that most of our modern ailments come from being forced to live unnatural lives that make our minds sick. You must take the steps towards becoming a WARRIOR and make sure to pass your lessons learned to your sons.

86.

Ancestor Worship

Before there was any centralized worship, religion was centered around individual families who worshipped the hearth fire and their ancestors above all else. The Greks referred to their home as their Fatherland, for it was where their ancestors were buried. They believed after death, the ancestors had to be cared for. They would often prepare an extra plate of food for the ancestors as they understood that if an ancestor starved in the afterlife, he would haunt them. Their dead ancestors transversed their properties and it was their duty to protect the land. No one other than family members could trespass onto their land.

Each day, a family gathered before its hearth fire for a meal and religious rites. The meals we share with our family today descend from this custom. The hearth fire itself was considered a God. More than that, it was a symbol of the family's survival and power. For the Patriarch, it brought great comfort to a man with heavy shoulders. It was the key to communing with the ancestors, it was a fond memory of being taught how to make fire by one's father, a powerful skill in the ancient world. Long after a man's father passed away, he was kept warm by the fire his father taught him to make.

We live in a time of disconnect from our ancestors and our bloodline's history. A lot of it comes from demoralization. Many fear knowing their family history. What if there were racist slaveholders in your bloodline? These beliefs are imposed upon you by your enemies. Your ancestors did what they had to do in order to survive and thrive in nature.

You as you are today are a continuation of an ancient bloodline that stretches back to the beginning of mankind. You are the PATRIARCH of this bloodline while you're alive. A Patriarch is more than just the head of a household. He was a priest of the family, a steward of his bloodline. Almost all peoples have had some form of ancestor worship. It exists in pure peoples who haven't been mindfucked by tyrants. You must remember WHO you are, and WHERE you come from. It's up to you to make sure your bloodline survives to the next generation and from there, your sons will continue the fight for survival. Remember all those who came before you and the sacrifices they made to make you possible.

87.

It's worth noting that when the Romans discovered the Jews, they thought the Jews were atheists. You had to be an atheist to only believe in one God. And we've spent the last thousand years only believing in one God. By the 1800s, Friedrich Nietzsche was proclaiming "God is dead." Perhaps, the Romans were right. The "major" religions of our time are dead husks compare to what they used to be. The biggest religion of our time is the religion of our enemies.

There's no going back to the glory days. No returning. We can only go forward and going forward, we must come to terms with the truth: we no longer know God. Is there one God or many Gods as believed by the Romans and all the other Aryan tribes? We don't know, but whatever the answer, there is a path left to us. A path back to God. We must become loved by God again.

What do we know about God? It seems naive to believe there is only one God that controls everything. Maybe there is a God for each race? We don't know. The Greks were more reasonable about such things. But since we do not know, we will continue to use the name God. God has left us a path, a Golden Path.

What is this path? The doctrines of nature. Throughout history, regardless of religion, the people who adhere to the doctrines of nature dominate, perpetuate, and expand. God rewards the people who master the doctrines of nature. Those that live in accordance with nature are on the Golden Path. Life ain't sunshine and rainbows. It's the fight for survival.

You have to keep pushing further into the unknown, into the frontier, to grow stronger. Might is Right is natural law. To survive and thrive, you have to be the best. This is the only true religion of mankind. The people that can stick to it become loved by God. They are living as God intended. How do we get back to the Golden Path? How do we build a foundation that can launch us into the frontier?

All Western people look back to the Greks as their point of origin. All Western people look back to the Roman Empire as something to strive for. There is reason for this. In these two ancient cultures, you get a visceral understanding of nature. Of what it takes to be the best. Some may not like this train of thought and feel like you have to be faithful to the complete history of your bloodline. And make no doubt, as I've said, bloodline is important.

But there is more to the equation. We all need inspiration. Every great man looked back to a hero that came before him. Alexander wanted to be like Herakles. Caesar strove to be better than Alexander. Napoleon sought to trump Caesar's conquests. The Warrior needs to internalize this. To have heroes you want to surpass. To see their stories as religious texts.

Am I saying you must imagine God as Zeus himself? No, the religious feeling the Greks and Romans had are gone. We don't know God, but we know the path he's left for us. That path has been traveled by the Greks and Romans. Ideas like the brotherhood of armed men is the foundation of a people comes from this Western point of origin. The Aryans expanded by way of military brotherhoods. Another aspect of these Aryan cultures is understanding that you have to give the franchise to men. If they have no incentives to be what they're meant to be, you have the civilization we have today.

To study the Western point of origin is to know God better. To know what he expects of his people. In these ancient peoples, you find the way back to the Golden Path.

88.

Fighting is the Warrior's Religion.

Strength and survival are the baseline values of a people. Without them, you die out. Men evolved to seek these baseline values at all costs. It takes great manipulation of the collective mind to get people to ignore these baseline values. You instill these values into your people, and they become clannish, tough, and ruthless. Manipulate it out of them and they become slaves. We evolved this way for a reason, to ignore it is to turn from the way of God.

Nietzsche made the bold claim that the modern man would shudder if he knew what the Greks really thought about Homer's *Iliad*. They loved the fighting, war, and adventure. They didn't see it as tragic, rather the heroes were doing what they could only dream of. It was instilled in the Greks that FIGHTING for one's city and tribe was the greatest honor. This was born out of the need for strength, in order to survive. We remember the Greks for their thought, but forget they were a SAVAGE people. They were constantly at war with each other and when the massive Persian Empire came along, thinking it could subject the small city-states to their rule, the Greks showed them brutality and ruthlessness on a scale they had never seen before.

Grek men trained from childhood to fight through contests. They were made to value the fight and the contest, in the same way, Americans are *made* to value blacks and gays. This life of ours is warfare, even now, when it seems like nothing ever happens and mankind seems to have mastered nature. Forget this truth at your own peril. Men were born to fight. Be who you're meant to be.

There is much mental sickness in our society, and it comes from not allowing men to be men. Men denied physical culture, not encouraged to fight and train for war, to not be allowed to follow their biological imperative, will grow depressed and develop these first-world mental illnesses. On the contrary, to take a sick man and direct him towards these ends will give him purpose. It will free him from his sickness. Training for war, striving for superiority, give man his ultimate purpose and allows a people to orient themselves towards the IDEAL values of power and supremacy. It is power and supremacy that will take man back to the frontier, back to the Golden Path of God.

You are made to live a certain way and God favors you when you do. The best at it become loved by God. A Warrior's excellence is proof of his devotion to God. Your people must make a constant effort to reinforce their baseline values in pursuit of their ideal values. What is meant by this? The brotherhood of armed men must be kept sacred at all costs. Racial cohesion forms the strongest bonds in a people, nothing can be allowed to break those bonds.

Success must be met with suspicion, always. Oswald Spengler said it was impossible for a people to maintain a heroic posture forever. When met with too much victory, too much glory, a people become decadent. They become soft; they lose their edge. A Warrior Religion must do its part to keep the people hard and strong. To always be oriented toward the frontier, where its disciples can test themselves against nature. Out there, on the frontier, is the path back to God. To abandon the frontier is to abandon the light of God. We must always strive for discomfort and challenge, to light the fire of God across the universe.

89.

"Mankind? It is an abstraction. There are, always have been, and always will be, men and only men." -Johann Wolfgang von Goethe

There are Men and Only Men

The brotherhood of armed men is the franchise. Without them, there can be no people, no tribe, no country. You — as a man — are a part of that franchise, whether you participate or not. Most boys become men with a shroud over their eyes, unable to see the true nature of the world. They experience what Friedrich Nietzsche called the transvaluation of all values in real-time. Their "virile instincts for war and victory" are hammered out of them at a young age under the unnatural

146

fluorescent lights of the classroom where their most formative years are wasted learning the virtues of the deformed. This will continue until men, and only men, choose freedom or as phrased by Nietzsche, "the will to be responsible for themselves."

The world you live in is an illusion, a mirage. One day, the mirage will reveal itself for what it really is: the barren desert, or it will trick you unto your death. The pity I have for the men who are tricked, who never see beyond the mirage, and are never given the opportunity to test themselves against nature. You see around you what Bronze Age Pervert described as "owned space." There are seemingly no more frontiers and very few opportunities for adventure. Instead, there is a massive apparatus we call the state that governs over your life and fences in the horizons. Despair is the most common emotion when the mirage fades.

I ask you not to despair, but to take a step back and observe the path before you. Yes, the road to victory is long and unforgiving. You will have to make yourself a warrior. It's worth noting that the Roman word for man was "VIR" which meant both warrior and hunter. The fight seems far above any one man, and it is, but you can take solace that you can fight it. You can even fly under the radar of our enemies long enough to deliver a thunderbolt that they never saw coming.

How? We are born under a vast empire. Over three hundred million people are living in the United States, on top of this, there are many vassal states of the empire that demand the attention of our enemies. But you must remember that you, as a man, are part of the franchise. Society is bound to the strength of the armed brotherhood. You can take steps to reclaim sovereignty without sticking your head up out of the dirt like a mole waiting to get whacked. The first step is recognizing that the world before you is not as it seems, and nature will one day destroy the illusion.

Your path, your duty to the blood, is to ensure the survival of your bloodline. To go beyond and find a way to thrive. To sit on top of the food chain. Modern society has attempted to deconstruct civilization into nothing. What's a man? What's a woman? An abstraction the leftist will tell you.

But men and women have roles to fill. They are made different for a reason. If the world fell tomorrow, you wouldn't have girl bosses and feminists. You — as a man — will get a chance, if the world fell. A chance to prove your worth to the world and God Himself, if you had been taking the right steps towards freedom. A woman's choices would depend on the man she had chosen. This is the way of the world.

90.

Man is the dominant primordial beast. He's seemingly risen to the top of the food chain, for now. But that may not always be so. The ones below you will always be vying for position, looking for their shot at the throne. Comfort and decadence have made us lose our edge. We've gotten soft. All efforts must be taken to undo the damage to our bloodlines.

Men are no simple creatures. Some of us are made for different tasks. Our world is complex, and it would be folly to leave behind all power and technics to our enemies, so you must play a dual role. On the one hand, you must re-embrace the virtues of survival that carried our ancestors to the top. You have to make yourself a more complete beast who, if the world fell tomorrow, will have a fighting chance. On the other, you have to vie for power and mastery of technics. It's a balancing act as we don't have the power to bend the world to our will. Be as prepared as you can for either scenario: the massive collapse of the state apparatus OR the capture of the state apparatus by our own.

Most want to bet on the fall and you should be preparing for it but recognize that our country is the strongest empire in the world. If our people can take the reins, fortune would be on our side. It is important to know both paths, to be able to take this gay empire and turn it into a vitalist IMPERIUM. It's beyond any one man to know all there is to know. That is for God and God alone, which is why the basic unit of mankind is the brotherhood of armed men. Each man in the brotherhood will have their strengths and weaknesses, and they must work together to survive and thrive. To these ends, you must make yourself worthy of the tribe and brotherhood for you do not understand the extent our enemies have gone to weaken our virile instincts.

Man is the dominant primordial beast, but he's spent generations getting softer, losing his edge. As man has gotten more technologically advanced, he's had to rely less on his physical prowess, but that doesn't make physical prowess any less vital to being a man. You must take note of everything that is killing your virile fighting power, as said by Teddy Roosevelt. How often are you outside? What kinds of foods are you eating? What materials are you handling? How often do you train?

How long was man a beast of the steppe? How long did he survive using his physical prowess and wits? Do you not think you're stunting your potential by avoiding exercise and nature? Do you not think that certain biological advantages get activated in the body when you do what you were made to do? There is a mindset shift that happens when you be who you're meant to be. Our minds work better when they're forced to contend with nature, with resistance. Man was not made to be a sedentary cow watching TV.

The first step is to go outside. You have no idea how harmful it is to be inside under unnatural lighting for days, years. Most of your time, ideally, should be spent outside. The sun is

POWER. The house, the job, are places of sickness. Your body needs fresh air and the sun. I would wager almost all men suffer from low testosterone and not being outside, in the sun, testing yourself has a lot to do with it.

The body and the mind thrive on the right kind of stress. You can only do what you can do, but you must strive for more. Keep pushing your limits. You should be rucking regularly, it's the standard for the modern Hoplite. Explore the world around you. Know what's out there in your local wilderness, off the roads.

91.

Barbaric Rites

Almost all Hollywood films are propaganda garbage. You're much better off spending your time reading the classics or the Aryan bible: the *Iliad*. Most born into this time, unfortunately, see a lot of movies and don't read the *Iliad* enough. Sometimes, however, these movies can contain nuggets of wisdom. Case in point: in the movie *Pirates of the Caribbean*, there is scene involving Johnny Depp's Jack Sparrow and the protagonist, Will Turner. He tells the Turner fellow, "The only rules that really matter are these: what a man can do, and what a man can't do." That one sentence encompasses the wisdom of the universe.

For instance, you can find some black on the street, kill them, wear his carved-off face as a mask, and cut off his right arm as sacrifice to the War God, but you can't control the police being called to hunt you down after the fact. Life is about making decisions. Decisions that fulfill your biological imperative to the blood. Primitive men didn't have to worry about the feds being called on them. If they wanted something, they took it, so long as they believed they could win or get away with it. This ranged from killing a man, raping a woman, stealing, to whatever else you could think of. Life ain't the fantasyland we're born into. That's a mirage in the desert, nothing more.

What happens when society collapses? Not if, but when. Oswald Spengler determined that cultures themselves were organisms that lived for around a thousand years. They had a spring, summer, fall, and winter or put another way, a childhood, adulthood, middle-aged, and old. Our civilization is named FAUSTIAN by Spengler, and he foresaw its end any time from now to another two centuries from now. It will happen and when it does, man will once again discover his Barbaric Rites. Are you ready for such an event? There are few who are.

I first heard the term "Barbaric Rites" from a fun workout account ran by Paul Waggener, but for me the term means something else. When I speak of Barbaric Rites, I speak of the religious, fanatical tendencies of the man forced back into nature. The last time we saw this was with our ancestors who were forced back into nature when they settled the New World. And what do you learn about these ancestors? You're made to believe that they were evil people who owned slaves and massacred the poor peaceful Indians. What you're not told is that the experience on the frontier was that of a racial Holy War. You're also not told how brutal the Indians were to the settlers and different Indian tribes. What would you have to do if the world fell tomorrow? What kind of barbarism would it take to survive? These are your Barbaric Rites. This is what your clan and family will ask of you, in order to survive.

They are the type of Rites you don't want to think about, but your ability to perform them better than your competition will make you loved by God. It will bestow upon you providence. They will give you the opportunity to do what few men have ever done: be remembered by mankind. Undying fame. Herakles is remembered by mankind, but was he the type of man our enemies would admire? No, he mutilated and killed people. Achilles is remembered by mankind. What did he do? He sacked cities and slaughtered men. He also, in the view of our leftist society, failed to fulfill his duty as a soldier by sitting out the war.

Life itself involves SAVAGE DECISIONS. You're made to believe that the good guys always win in the end, but what if the opposite is true? What if your country isn't the mighty bald eagle in the sky, but a chthonic octopus creature wrapping its tentacles over the whole earth? What kind of hero could destroy such a monster? Nature is cruel. The nice guy never makes it out on top. You have to be willing to do what it takes to win, to follow the Barbaric Rites as God intended.

It's important to understand that man is a beast in nature. He isn't some higher organism. He may be the top dog of the earth, for now, but that may not always be so. You have to become the dominant primordial beast. You must train the exerting of your WILL. It ain't enough to have a will for something more. You must impose your will on the world. Impose it on your enemies and break their wills. Become a breaker of wills.

You make these savage decisions, hold fast to the Barbaric Rites, and master the conditions you are born into. Look further beyond, to the next frontier. Impose your will and grow stronger. The Barbaric Rites belong to men only. Men only are capable of doing what it takes. It's what we're born to do. What we're built to do. Otherwise, there would be no difference between the sexes.

You must use the Barbaric Rites to get that red blood surging in your veins. Rev the engines. Pursue the Great Work and leave your mark on the world. Be great enough at it and you will turn the wheel of mankind. Do not get comfortable, and do not fall into hubris. Always keep your eyes on the frontier.

The place where growth happens, where you can keep your teeth sharp.

"He who does more, is worth more." -Geoffroi de Charny

92.

Long Live the Hoplite

In ancient times, the Grek Hoplite did not have federal funding. He was not provided with armor or shield or spear. The Hoplite had to provide his own armor and weapons. The cost of his equipment was equated to the cost of buying a truck today. Now most people buy cars, most of the time, however, it's on credit. The Hoplite was well off enough to provide his own equipment and maintain it. In the off-season, he was a farmer and a citizen of his city. It's believed that this alliance forged by the brotherhood of armed men was the origin of the Republic form of government. It wasn't a democracy as you had to be well off enough to participate.

In our modern day, you sign military contract, and the government provides you with everything you need. You need only do your duty for your country. The problem is manyfold. We have an all-volunteer force so not all-American men are made to be warriors(as they should be). Remember what Nietzsche said, "The free man is a warrior." And we supposedly live in the land of the free. You must have the will to be responsible for yourself.

My fren BANE on twatter is leading the way on what I believe is the RIGHT path for the American man in our time. Bane says that if you want to remain on this sinking ship we call the United States, you have to become a modern Hoplite and the best way to do this is to join your local national guard unit as infantry. The amount of money you need for all the equipment necessary for a modern Hoplite is — thankfully — still the same. It's around the cost of a truck. You need a plate carrier,

153

plates, a helmet, night vision, thermal vision, and of course rifles and ammo. Let's not forget the important things like friends and training. When you see what it takes to be a Hoplite, you see why Bane's advice of joining the national guard is your best option, but if you don't want to do that, you have a lot of work ahead of you to prove your devotion to the War God. It's not just having the equipment, but getting the training, and forging alliances.

93.

What I want to go over next is WHY Bane's recommendations are what you should be working towards no matter where you are in life. If you read a man like Oswald Spengler, you learn that the civilization we're a part of, the Faustian civilization, is inextricably tied to technics. Look at how much war has evolved from the wars of Napoleon to the two World Wars. The scales have turned so much against the Warrior and infantryman, why would I suggest this as the ideal? How can the modern Hoplite deal with drones, air strikes, and the like? Hell, you might get nuked into oblivion before you even get a chance to fight. Fortune must be on your side.

The reality is that we are in FAUSTIAN civilization, not Faustian culture. If Spengler's timetables are correct, we're already in the winter of our culture's shelf life. What's going to happen when we don't have the men capable of piloting planes or making drones? Or fast forward to some apocalyptic scenario where the state falls. Faustian man will have lost all the skills that got him to where he is. The fighting man, however, will always be necessary. He will always be useful. You want to learn those skills to make yourself ready and pass them down to your sons as BARBARIC RITES.

At some point, a new culture is going to take hold. What it is, we don't know. What we do know is the doctrines of nature are the laws of God. Those that can adhere to the laws of God will get their way back to the top. Our forefathers who founded the

United States were the last people forced back into nature and this experience transformed them. It changed them from their European cousins. It's our duty to the blood to make sure our descendants will be ready for a similar journey and that they are ready for an even more ambitious vision of Manifest Destiny.

It's the Manifest Destiny for our race to leave Earth. To spread to the stars. Many things must happen before we can do this. There must be a powerful foundation built for our people to retake power. Part of this is making every American man a modern Hoplite devoted to God. Putting ourselves in a position to either take power when the opportunity arises or be out of threat areas should the world go nuclear and collapse upon itself. In either scenario, the ideal is to spread Manifest Destiny over the earth so that can securely take mankind to the next level: the stars.

This starts on the individual level, with you, with me. You must be building towards this ideal of the Hoplite. Joining the national guard or seeking out training. Making friends and forging brotherhoods along the way. Creating bastions of strength within this empire. There is much work to be done. This is not something that will likely be realized in our lifetimes, and you have to look beyond yourself. You're only a steward of your bloodline while alive. Your duty to the blood is to move the bar.

You may not be able to control when the world falls, but you can control your own little microcosm. Your own war band. The foundation of a people is the brotherhood of armed men.

LONG LIVE THE INFANTRY

94.

Fervor Dreams

The only thing that is certain is war. Life is war. It is the passage to manhood and glory. War is the only way out. This is why so much effort has been done to soften and pacify the American. To make him comfortable and plump while he's milked for all he's worth. Power is never surrendered; it must be taken.

A Warrior Religion is the vessel in which you can take back that power. Soft lands make for soft people. You must make the conscious decision to seek out the hard, the worst environments imaginable to strengthen your resolve. To see if you're really alive. You must seek out ritual hardship in fighting, surviving, and strength to correct the course. To master your conditions on this earth. The warlike and manly frontier spirit must be awakened in our men. The overriding desire to become a mother awakened in our women.

This is how a people survives. How they build empires that last thousands of years. War is always certain. The strength of a race is how warlike their men are, and how quickly their women replace the losses in war. The two sexes must work together in this Great Task. This should be the heart of a new Warrior Religion and the foundation from which our secret covenant enters this world.

The strongest Warrior Religions come out of hard peoples. The Spartans need no explanation. The Romans were surrounded by enemies on all sides and had to fight for their place in the world. The Christians came out of the arid desert to take control of the Roman Empire. The Germans in both World Wars were a dominating fighting force that forced the rest of the world to unite to defeat them. The vicious Chechen mountain peoples are a more recent example of a Warrior Religion. Where will the enclaves of a new Warrior Religion form in the United States? How will they forge hard men?

Warrior rituals, warrior culture. This is where the focus turns to the man wanting more out of this life, the man who wants to see the end of this leftist hellscape. Fighting, surviving, and strength are the concerns of the disciple. Fire and fanaticism drive him onwards. Those who aren't warriors, but who are fanatical to the cause, orient themselves in a way that assists the warrior, that helps make him superior. In this way, they work together to make the religion and race superior. Warfare in the modern day is complex and requires many types of men.

War is the Father of all. It's your duty to yourself, your family, and your people to make yourself a warrior. To be responsible for the freedom of you and yours. This is how you would devote yourself to a new Warrior Religion and its secret covenant. To sow the seeds of destruction into this false world. It's how you devote yourself to LIFE. Physical culture and the way of the warrior fulfill man's purpose more than anything else on this earth.

95.

Men of race and power take oaths to one another. Swearing to keep their Sacred Fires lit, to keep their old bloodlines, bloodlines that have existed since the beginning of time, going for eternity. Removing themselves from the culture of guilt that the modern world wants to impose upon them and creating their own cultures built around honor and shame because that is what nature intended. Nature is savage and enteral, so too, we must be warlike and manly. We must be primitive, closer to the darkness, prepared to deal with the evil the leviathan plans to throw our way. Men of frontier spirit.

The mastery of space and conditions fuels a man's will to power. It's up to a Warrior Religion to inspire this drive in its disciples. For the men themselves to inspire it in each other. To devote themselves to rituals that help them to accomplish these ends. This sentiment is found in our deepest blood-nature. It's what you're born to do. The mass sickness and depression in our people come from listening to the snakes in our society preaching leftism.

You have to believe what I already know: you are chosen. Why else are you being targeted by the world? They fear your power, your potential. They fear the truth. You must become what they fear. Become the boogeyman under their bed. The white devil waiting for them in the darkness.

Fear is a tool. Your enemies use fear against you every day, it's time you turn it against them.

PART FOUR:
AMERICAN PATRICIANS

96.

Promethean Virtue

A new Warrior Religion should acknowledge the Unknown God, for as a people, we've strayed too far from the Golden Path to know the divine. We acknowledge however, different peoples at different times have known the divine. One of which is the Ancient Greks who we trace back as the origin point of Western peoples. As origin, the Greks leave behind wisdom in a manner we can understand and make use of. This world we live in can be seen in the Nietzschean concept of the Dionysian but gone off the rails. Those who find their way to our side do so with an Apollonian desire to bring order to the chaos. But to embrace just the Apollonian desire for order is to set yourself up for wholesale destruction.

You must understand that our enemies are not honorable creatures. They are rats and worms. They will pull out all the stops for the chance to stab you in the back without ever presenting a target. What you're up against is the antithesis of the noble excellence you saw in ancient Aryan warlords. What you realize is even they, are a part of nature. Might IS right, in whatever form it takes. So where does that put the Apollonian man who seeks the favor of The Gods?

You must realize that with the lion is always the fox. The Ancient Greks knew this to be true, which is why you saw in their culture the domination of the Titans by the Olympians. Even after the Aryan conquests took place, there were still cults devoted to the old Gods. There's no ridding the world of either of these forces. In the Sacred Fire, I talked about the story of PROMETHEUS, an important Grek myth about how man came to harness fire. They saw their mastery over fire as a crime against nature. A terrible sacrilege. This crime could not go unpunished, so Prometheus has his liver eaten out every day by eagle.

Nietzsche examines this aspect of Grek culture in his book *The Birth of Tragedy*. He uses example of Oedipus who solves the riddle of the sphinx, but his great wisdom is seen as a crime against nature and so he is punished by unknowingly killing his father and then, marrying his mother. Great wisdom is a terrible crime against nature. This is how the primitive man saw it. The "Titanic striving individual" as Nietzsche put it, must commit sacrilege in his pursuit of the Great Work. He goes on further to talk about how the "best and highest blessing" attained by man was obtained through this sacrilege and man must in turn accept the consequences.

Noble man harnessing fire in his attempt to reach the heights of Mount Olympus, to give himself the ability to destroy even The Gods, had to be punished with eternal suffering. Acquiring complete control of fire was seen by the first men as the "plundering of divine nature." This may sound confusing or mysterious, and perhaps it is, what you must understand is this knowledge is vital to fighting the enemy. This divine plundering of fire by man is directly related to the Semitic myth of the fall. Nietzsche explains that the sin of the Semitic fall is seen as passive and female, whereas the sin of controlling fire was seen as active and manly. There is a better "ethical background" to the Promethean virtue of harnessing fire. The evil of controlling fire is what led to human guilt and suffering.

It's not enough to be Apollonian, to strive for order and nobility when some rat can take you out from behind the scenes. The complete man must utilize the lion as well as the fox. As he Titanically strives, he must see both the Olympian world of nature and order and its dark Titanic underbelly of the scorned and deformed. To do anything great, to leave your mark on the world will require your willingness to enter the Titanic underworld. To go into the darkness. And you will be made to pay the consequences.

97.

The Titanic Striving Man

The enemy cannot be conquered with the Apollonian or Olympian spirit alone. You must make yourself a more complete man. The Greks saw Prometheus giving fire to man as a crime worth eternal torment, but if pay attention, Zeus did not take fire back from man. He did not punish man for acquiring control over fire. Zeus did not end his experiment, man. Man was left to turn fire against nature, to dominate the planet. Perhaps, The Gods expected it from man.

Nature isn't some kind-hearted, traditionalist farmer. Nature is Titanic and barbaric. It requires you to compete with all other creatures, in an eternal war to reach the top of the mountain of power. The Gods understood this when they fought the Titans in the Titanomachy. They understood the reality of nature: do not lose wars. Zeus grievously punished the Titans for opposing him and made sure they would never rise again. It ain't as simple as good vs evil. You have to want victory more than the enemy and be willing to do whatever it takes to obtain it.

To what depths are you willing to descend to win? How low into the underworld will you go to be a Prometheus to man? To give your people the power to overcome. War in nature has only one rule: you must win. Everything else is on the table, but you must win. Titanic striving and barbarism will become necessary for you to fight against an enemy that seeks to destroy you without ever presenting a target. You cannot stand like a sitting target waiting for them to face you, you must enter the shadows and hunt your enemies down.

This path is not for the weak of heart, which is why Nietzsche referred to it as both Dionysian and tragic. Those willing to enter the underworld may disfigure their souls in the fight. That is tragic, but losing is a far worse fate. There is redemption to be found in this path. To be the conquerors of the occupational class requires sacrifice on levels not yet comprehended by our people. Remember the frontier barbarism the early Americans had to embrace to tame the wilderness and win the racial Holy War.

You will not usher in the return of the OLYMPIANS until you first master the underworld with Promethean virtue. Strive for superiority and through superiority, through embracing tragedy, you will bring myth back into the world. A return to the age of heroes.

98.

"Regarded more closely, it is war which produces these results, war in favour of liberal institutions, which, as war, allows the illiberal instincts to subsist. For war trains men to be free. What in sooth is freedom? Freedom is the will to be responsible for ourselves. It is to preserve the distance which separates us from other men. To grow more indifferent to hardship, to severity, to privation, and even to life itself. To be ready to sacrifice men for one's cause, one's self included. Freedom denotes that the virile instincts which rejoice in war and in victory, prevail over other instincts; for instance, over

the instincts of 'happiness.' The man who has won his freedom, and how much more so, therefore, the spirit that has won its freedom, tramples ruthlessly upon that contemptible kind of comfort which tea-grocers, Christians, cows, women, Englishmen and other democrats worship in their dreams. The free man is a warrior." -Friedrich Nietzsche

What it Means to be an American Patrician

In Friedrich Nietzsche's *Twilight of the Idols*, he has what I believe to be one of his most important passages, entitled "My Concept of Freedom." Red-blooded Americans like to talk about how they live in the "land of the free and the home of the brave," meanwhile their leaders are imposing some of the most tyrannical policies imaginable. Compare our current tax rate to what our forefathers in the Revolutionary rebelled against. The taxes imposed upon the colonists were measly in comparison to what we put up with today. It would be one thing if this taxation was used for the American people, but no, it's used instead to put a foot on the throat of the American people. How many thousands, if not millions, of immigrants, have we allowed to cross our southern border? How many immigrants did we bring back from Afghanistan — a war we started and neglected to finish — for we could not make the country safe for the Afghanis who were rushing to get aboard the last flights out of the country? Do you honestly think, as an American, you are free?

Americans are the pay pigs of a gay and hostile empire. The empire exists on the backs of the men it's trying, with all its might, to suppress. Every day, Americans are made to take part in intellectually dishonest arguments made solely to limit the freedoms of Americans due to the emergence(only within the last generation or so, I might add) of bad actors taking advantage of the FREEDOMS our ancestors fought and died for. Our enemies would have you believe the founding fathers

163

would have banned automatic weapons because of their ability to kill when these same founding fathers had just finished waging the War for Independence against the strongest empire in the world at the time. If the American Revolution happened in the modern era with the same founding fathers, I promise you they wouldn't think the modern weapons of war were too dangerous for their people to have. They would still believe it was the RIGHT of the American to bear arms, to protect him and his family from tyranny — foreign or domestic. The only mistake they made is not making the right to bear arms as more than a right, but a trait of our race, a part of our religion and living constitution.

The government has an interest in your children. They are, after all, the future taxpayers of this corrupt regime, and you see this more in the news. You hear more and more about teachers helping their students become trans behind the backs of the children's parents. There are even stories of parents being forced to allow their children to undergo sex change or have child protective services take their children away. Even more tales of parents being unable to stop their divorced spouse from letting their children undergo this mutilation. Why is this so? The more people the state — again, the coldest of cold monsters — can convince to convert to their woke ideology, the more agreeable slaves they create.

It was said that during the RONA "pandemic" of 2020 gays were the most compliant with covid measures. They were more likely to get vaccinated and revaccinated than any other group. This psychological warfare is waged by the state against its subjects to mold them into the perfect pay pigs. Cows to be milked for all their worth. Leave behind these "marginalized" groups(who are really preferred groups) and look at America's obesity rate. Two-thirds of Americans are obese. What have we become but cows to be milked?

The type of people the state selects for do not value freedom. They value comfort, security, and fantasies of how the world actually works. More than anything, these people selected for by the state are CONFORMISTS. They will do anything daddy tells them to do which is why they are so highly valued by our gangster class which claims to support "liberal democracy." These people are also a liability because they are weak. You can't depend on them to physically support the empire. The state, in turn, must also try to recruit from amongst the American race, fighting men they can use up to give their corrupt gangster class a little more time. For our own side, you can't depend on them to do the right thing. To not be cowards.

If you are interested in becoming an American PATRICIAN, you have to see this happening all around you. It should disgust you, but most importantly, it should be teaching you lessons. What the state gives you freely, is not free. They exact a toll that may be taken from you or your descendants down the line. You must become responsible for yourself and your family and do what you can to lessen the power of the state.

The way you do this is manyfold. You have to live in a way that allows you to be independent. You have to be able to prevent indoctrination against your family. You have to be a modern Hoplite and warrior. There must be brotherhoods formed with your fellow Patricians and these alliances must be used to increase your tribe's overall power. This is not some quick fix to the problems before us. There are many obstacles to be overcome.

The biggest one is the civil rights act that prevents Americans from exercising their right to freedom of association. What freedom of association is in our time is ethnic nepotism. All the foreigners and grifters in this country can practice nepotism unabated, the law isn't for them. It's for us. I tell you now to be nepotistic. Favor your own above all others but be smart about it. Keep it in the shadows, under the nose of our enemies. Don't broadcast it.

You need to be gathering Patricians of various skillsets into your tribe to take the place of the state. In the ideal world, you would all live close together, but I realize that this is almost impossible in the modern day. It's something you and your descendants, however, must work towards. There are no 30-day pills out of this. We are in a struggle that will last generations. These are the steps you must take if you want to be truly free. Nature is savage and eternal; you must do as Nietzsche said and make yourself a warrior who doesn't depend on the state for his protection or the protection of his family.

99.
"The decision over war and peace is the highest sovereign prerogative." -Ernst Jünger

The reality of nature is the cream always rises to the top which is why you must not fall into a victim mentality. Why you must strive for superiority, strive for ARISTEIA in whatever you set out to do. To be truly free is to be SOVEREIGN and as Ernst Jünger says, only a sovereign can choose between war and peace. If you cannot decide to go to war, you are not free.

A man not in complete control of his life can be manipulated which is why our gangster class purports all these seemingly "humane" ideas like dem programs, welfare, and credit. You must show that you are your own man. That you can stand on your own. That you're not thrall to the state. This is your way to freedom and sovereignty. Pursue excellence to make the state yours. As such, begin thinking of yourself as sovereign. Make the mental change now and the physical change will follow.

You are sovereign. You control the decision between war and peace now. You can choose to chimp out and go out ignobly, but that would be in contradiction to both your duty to your blood as a Patrician and overall victory in this Holy War. And yes, we have been born into a HOLY WAR. To obtain victory in this Holy War will require you to pursue Virtù.

100.

Virtù, not virtue.

The word virtue has been completely destroyed in our time. What is virtue? What does it mean to be virtuous? In our time, it means to be good, nice, kind, among other things. To have character and do the right thing.

Where does virtue come from? Its origin is Latin. It comes from the Roman word VIRTUS. It was also pronounced differently: weer-toos, not ver-tus. The VIR in virtus stood for man. In Ancient Rome, a male was not automatically made a man once he reached a certain age. He had to undergo a rite of passage, show spiritedness. He had to exercise his will.

Virtus itself doesn't have the modern connotations we give the word virtue today. For the Romans, it meant MANLINESS. How manly a Roman was earned him virtus.

Virtù is a concept from Niccolo Machiavelli that was based on Roman virtus. It meant MARTIAL EXCELLENCE and POWER of a man or people. It also encompasses ALL the necessary traits for accomplishing those ends. Machiavelli listed pride, bravery, skill, forcefulness, and the ability to be ruthless when necessary, as traits of Virtù.

Leave behind the watered-down concept of virtue. Embrace instead Virtù. In a Warrior Religion, fighting is religion and through manifesting virtu, you show your devotion to God.

101.

The Human Type Required

What is the human type required for the prosperity of a martial people? What does it take to hold onto it? Now I say humans, instead of just men because women share a part in that franchise.

The brotherhood of armed men is the franchise. It's the foundation of any people. I hold to that, but as with almost everything on this earth, there's more to the story. If the war band represents the franchise and foundation of a people, the FAMILY is the franchise and foundation of the warrior. Much of the most meaningful work you could be doing for your people right now is foundation building. If you have the reach to influence more than this, you absolutely should do so, but for most of our people, the path is rebuilding the foundation forged by our ancestors. Now I may be accused of being called trad after this, but I think these steps are VITAL to man and the development of martial peoples.

There are many on the right who long for the return of piracy and the mannerbund. The reality is that the world has grown infinitely more complex the longer mankind lives on this earth and it will continue to become harder. The onus is on you to get stronger, to meet this challenge. Strive for superiority over your enemies. Life itself is the climb up the mountain of power. And then if you can reach the top, it's beating anyone who comes to take a shot at the king. This is what life is and what it always will be.

A martial people must never lose sight of their purpose. A martial people don't become martial for the sake of being warriors, they become martial to survive, to ensure the survival of their bloodlines. It goes back to keeping your family alive, to make sure you instill in your children the desire to carry on the fight, to make the family stronger from generation to generation, and to conquer your enemies. What does it take to survive? This is something Americans especially, have lost sight of. Our ancestors knew it like the back of their hands as they tried to survive in the New World. You don't have to go back very far in the history of our race to see the hardness of our ancestors.

Maybe up to when, say, the War Between the States? Even shortly past that time, Americans had the WILL to be responsible for themselves. Self-reliance in extremis. How many Americans think about what it took their ancestors in say, the 1800s, to survive? What skills did they have that we completely lack today? It goes beyond what God you pray to, what values you have. If the world fell tomorrow, how long could you keep your family alive?

If the world fell tomorrow, how long could you hold out with the food in your house? Do you even own land or a house? Could you defend your home if it was attacked? Imagine being in a city — a reality for most Americans. What would you do to survive? Do you have friends you could count on? What could you do now, today? Everyone likes to dream about what they would do when the world fell, but how many know, the skills, and the training to survive?

You look back to the American of the 1800s, what do you think your average eighteen-year-old knew that almost no one knows today? You have to get military survival training just to learn what the average 1800s American family already knew how to do. Maybe you don't have to get military training, but you're paying good money to get this kind of training that should have been taught to you by your parents and family. Now, what kind of skills and knowledge are we talking about? Could you perform the Promethean birthright of all men and make fire in the wilderness? How many men could do this without the aid of modern technology? Would you know what kind of wood to even look for?

Could you make an axe to even chop the wood? We're talking about the most primitive man type of skills, but the reality is you need an axe to make society. There is a massive skills gap between modern man and his 1800s American ancestors. People want to argue that these types of things don't matter anymore. We've moved beyond this. Our technology is so much more advanced. This is the Grek HUBRIS at work.

There will be a fall. There are no indicators that nothing is getting better. When the fall will happen is anyone's guess, but it is coming. How prepared are you for it? Can you do this primitive man stuff? I haven't even got into hunting. Could you go out into the wilderness and even hunt for food? There are many, many skills the average American lacks today that were vital only two hundred years ago.

The average American kid from the 1800s was shown how to survive in the wilderness. They were shown how to hunt for food, how to prepare that food. Shown how to make fire. How to shoot a gun and defend himself. He was shown how to build, even how to make tools in order to build. We think we're so far ahead of our ancestors, but we have terrible weaknesses that allow us to be exploited. We have become pay pigs, sheep to be sheared, cows to be milked.

Self-reliance, self-reliance, and I'll say it again, self-reliance. Nietzsche said that the free man had to have the will to be responsible for himself. If you want to take on the current king atop the mountain of power, you had better be a more complete man. Your war band had better be made up of complete men. In the complete man, you get the Titanic and barbaric striving man who gained mastery over fire and conquered the world.

The warrior's foundation is his family. I promote my fren BANE's advice of joining the military if you can, to learn these skills, but these skills have to be taken back to the tribe, to the family. Your children should be learning as toddlers what you had to learn as an adult. This HOLY WAR of ours will extend beyond our lifetimes and our children must be better men. It starts with you and your woman choosing not to be just another example of the WEAK human type you see in modern America today. You both have to realize that having children is far from a selfish decision, but a holy act. You should be aiming to have large families, building brotherhoods and communities your family can depend on when the going gets tough.

Only by taking these steps can Americans take the reins of this empire. Only by this path may you reach the summit of the mountain of power can cast your enemies over the mountainside.

102.
"What we do here is going to have generational consequences." -Frank Kitson

Generational Consequences

A British Army Officer, Frank Kitson, regarding the conflict with Northern Ireland, commented, "What we do here is going to have generational consequences." Moderns do not think in this way. The neocons did not think like this when they chose to invade Iraq and Afghanistan. Our current politicians in government do not think like this. They see only the here and now. Almost all Americans think in the here and now. They're figuring out how to get theirs. To find a way to make it.

Older generations of Americans had the same mentality, and it was fostered in them by their families. The America they grew up in was a different America than the one we live in today. In a way, it was an America for Americans. Yes, you had to be thrown out there to make your own way, to pick yourself up by your bootstraps, and oftentimes, it worked because that's what the country required at the time. We don't live in the same America and different strategies are necessary. You have to look beyond yourself, about how you can set up your descendants for a better life than you had. Don't give into the resentment instilled in most Americans about how they've been screwed over by the boomers. It's an easy thing to do, but it doesn't help you.

Most of us alive today were raised by parents who understood the old America and didn't prepare us properly for the world as it is. You cannot make the same mistake with your children. And on the subject of children, you absolutely cannot be the ignoble end of your bloodline. Many are disheartened at the prospect of having children. Remember, you've had ancestors that have been through much worse. You owe a duty to the blood to have children and set them up as best you can. You are more knowledgeable about the problems facing our people than your parents were and must act accordingly.

Think of yourself now as a PATRIARCH. You are steward of a bloodline that stretches back to the beginning of mankind. You must take care that your family gets a better opportunity than you did. The actions you take in life have generational consequences as do the actions of your parents and grandparents. Do your part to get your family on the right course. The best excel no matter the time they're born into. Do not let the times be an excuse.

You have to make yourself hard for the times to come. You have to make your children harder. The foundation you didn't have must be built for the prosperity of your family and its bloodline. This isn't what most people want to hear. They want money or a way out. There is no way out so long as you choose to remain American. Your only way out is through.

Think about the generational consequences when you make decisions about your life. The decisions you make will stretch beyond your own life. How can you start moving towards BETTER instead of drowning in the inertia of the modern age? You hear all the time about how millennials and zoomers will be unable to own a house. How can you be the exception?

If you've made mistakes, who hasn't? Not all your ancestors were thoroughbred. Not all of them made the right decisions. You must correct course, no matter where you are on the journey. At the very best, you will be a testament to what a man can do, and at the very worse, your children will be better prepared to face the trials ahead. This must be your mentality going forward. Think generationally. Our enemies make their money on you thinking only in terms of your own life. Disappoint them.

103.
The White Whale and Herman Melville's Prophecy of Power

Herman Melville's *Moby Dick* is the American epic. The central character is Ismael with whom we learn about the world of whaling. He first meets the cannibal Queequeg, the son of a South Sea chieftain who is tattooed and Pagan harpooner. After a mix-up before bed, they become friends and swear oaths of friendship to each other. They sign up to go on the Pequod's next voyage. The Pequod becomes a conglomerate of all the races. Queequeg a Polynesian, along with a negro, and an Indian are all harpooners of the Pequod. Pagans and Christians gathered under the command of the Quaker Captain Ahab.

After the voyage takes off, we must wait some time to get a look at our Captain. He's hidden away somewhere brooding. But eventually, he emerges to give the crew a speech. We learn that his ivory leg is the result of his last encounter with the mystical White Whale, MOBY DICK. A creature even the Pagan harpooners knew of. He bids them to keep their eyes open, always be on the lookout for the White Whale.

The Pequod conquers many leviathans, but the White Whale is always a step ahead, evading their pursuit. Ahab asks every ship they come across, "Have you seen the White Whale?" Ahab is a man of immense, focused, purity of purpose. There is only Moby Dick and it is his Great Task to rid the world of his tyranny. The Quaker in Ahab has him set on a Holy Crusade. He suffered a grievous injury at the hands of the White Whale and it's his job to make sure it doesn't happen to anyone else. Other ship captains, his first mate Starbuck, all try to dissuade him from this hunt — they all try, in vain.

Then on a fated night, amidst a terrible storm, Ahab calls the crew together to perform a barbaric rite. Using thunder-fire and dark magic, he seduces the men to take up his Holy War against the White Whale. Everyone— including our Ismael the narrator — gets caught up in the zeal of the hunt, everyone but the first mate Starbuck. When I first read Moby Dick, I too, got caught up in Ahab's Crusade. I said, "YES! That's RIGHT." I saw his WAR against the Whale as right and just.

Moby Dick was spotted soon after that night and the chase lasted for three days. It was a valiant struggle. By the last day, one of the harpooners is lashed to the flank of the White Whale. Angered by this assault upon him, Moby Dick sinks the Pequod, everyone going down bravely with the ship. Ahab tries for the last time to slay Moby Dick on the last boat, but the wire of his harpoon gets tied around his neck in the attack and The White Whale pulls him into the depths. Never to be seen again. All the crew is gone, save for our Ismael, who was knocked off Ahab's boat at the final moment. Spared the fate of the crew.

104.

*"But it is a great book, a very great book, the greatest book of
the sea ever written. It moves awe in the soul. The terrible
fatality. Fatality. Doom. Doom! Doom! Doom! Something
seems to whisper it in the very dark trees of America. Doom!
Doom of what? Doom of our white day."* -D.H. Lawrence

The Pequod represents America.

It was long after I read the book that I came across a passage
about *Moby Dick* and Herman Melville from D.H. Lawrence.
It inspired me to read the chapter he had on the great novel in
his book, *Studies in Classic American Literature*. This passage
completely changed how you read Melville. Before Lawrence, I
saw Ahab's Crusade as glorious. It was a glorious death for the
captain, something the Ancient Greks would resonate with. It
was man's battle against nature. A battle we must ultimately
lose, but a battle we must face with honor. When you first read
Lawrence's study of Moby Dick, however, you're left with
despair. Despair for America.

Somehow in 1851, Melville saw America sinking like the
Pequod. The Pequod was the ship of diversity. The Christian
Ismael becomes brothers with the cannibal Pagan Queequeg.
The ship recruits all the races on board to go after the White
Whale. All united in the grand campaign of the Quaker,
Captain Ahab. A campaign for vengeance, but it's more than
vengeance. Ahab has within him a sentiment we all know and
detest today: the progressive zeal.

It's not enough that Moby Dick spared Ahab the first time.
Ahab has to go on his Crusade to make sure no one else has to
suffer like he did. One time is too many. We all know this
sentiment. It's the leftist mind at work when they rail against
gun violence or accusations of racism. Ahab — like the leftist
— truly believes he can make the world better. That he can
change nature itself. He must make the sea behave and

embrace liberal democracy. The White Whale exists as an affront to Ahab.

D.H. Lawrence however, leaves keen insights on the mind of Melville, as well as an unintentional prophecy of power for a Warrior Religion. Yes, that's right a prophecy of power! You can look at the Pequod as America and you should. It's prophetic in a way, all the races gathered together under common purpose: to conquer the White Man. At head of this alliance is the White Man himself, seeking to conquer his very nature. By conquering himself, he dooms himself.

105.

"What then is Moby Dick? He is the deepest blood-being of the white race; he is our deepest blood-nature. And he is hunted, hunted, hunted by the maniacal fanaticism of our white mental consciousness. We want to hunt him down. To subject him to our will. And in this maniacal conscious hunt of ourselves we get dark races and pale to help us, red, yellow, and black, east and west, Quaker and fire-worshipper, we get them all to help us in this ghastly maniacal hunt which is our doom and our suicide. The last phallic being of the white man. Hunted into the death of upper consciousness and the ideal will. Our blood- self subjected to our will. Our blood-consciousness sapped by a parasitic mental or ideal consciousness." -D.H. Lawrence

It's a mistake to despair about the sinking of the Pequod, you're not supposed to be on the Pequod. You're supposed to be the Great White Beast.

D.H. Lawrence believes his fate to be on the Pequod, but if you read his review of *Moby Dick*, you realize Melville left behind a prophecy of power. The Pequod in all of its strength and diversity is felled by the Great White Beast, Moby Dick who Lawrence also calls the white man's "deepest blood-being" and "deepest blood-nature." Furthermore, Moby Dick is the "upper consciousness and the ideal will." The White Men hunting Moby Dick have their "blood-consciousness sapped by a parasitic mental or ideal consciousness." Often, I've described America as being run by parasites. Perhaps Lawrence too, recognized this.

It's a mistake to despair over the sinking of the Pequod, the sinking of America. You're not supposed to be on the Pequod. You're supposed to be the Great White Beast, Moby Dick. Moby Dick is your deepest blood-being, your deepest blood-nature. He is the ideal will. And what is the White Whale, but a force of nature? He is the White Man as he should be, living in accordance with nature. Dominating and world-conquering. Not even America can bring him to heel.

Many Americans have felt nothing but despair for a long time. Their country has been stolen from them. There's been seemingly no hope for the future. No charted path out of hell. Lawrence despairs with you. This isn't your fate, however. Your fate is with Moby Dick. That is your charted course. To become a force of nature beyond the "strength and diversity" of liberal democracy. To become the Great White Beast.

This is the prophecy of power left to White men by Herman Melville. There is nothing but the dark depths of the ocean should you choose to remain on The Pequod. But should you make yourself like the Great White Beast, you will find victory and your blood should continue through the ages. Long after The Pequod is forgotten. Embrace your blood-being, your blood-nature. Do not shy away from it. Do not get seduced by the self-destructive zeal of Ahab.

This is your path. To become the boogeyman. To become Moby Dick, the Great White Beast. Power lies with the RACE, not the nation.

106.

To be born into this world is to be born to a race. No matter how good or sweet the enemy's idea of some colorblind society is, in all of human history it's never existed. Each race is distinct and unique from their counterparts. It took different strategies for these races to survive, but one thing they all shared in common is the distrust of those who aren't them. When all the niceties and comforts disappear, man always falls back to his racial groups for protection. You must have this racial consciousness, to be able to see that those of the same race will favor each other over other races. Perhaps, the White Man's greatness can be attributed to his ability to see past race, to imagine something better, but we have also seen that it doesn't lead to better. It opens the Pandora's Box of our annihilation.

You have to begin thinking of yourself as part of a collective. No, you don't have to like everyone in your race. No one does, but when the chips are down, you'd much rather be ruled over by your own than by some other race that hates you. At least your own has some idea of preserving the race. In this world you're born into, your race is being hunted and as such, you have to tighten up. Take care of your own, but don't broadcast it. Don't put yourself in any position where the race has to burn resources to get you out of trouble.

Racial consciousness is vital for everything that comes next. You can't choose how you were born, but this society wants you to hate your blood. Never, never buy into their anti-White vitriol. Use all this hatred as a synthesis for powerful racial cohesion. The basic unit of mankind isn't the individual man. It's the brotherhood of armed men that makes up the ranks of nations, tribes, and clans. This is how you effect change in the world.

Being HUNTED means you have to hold yourself and your race to a higher standard. You can't present openings for our enemies to capitalize on. You can't commit tactical blunders that put your people in a bad position. You have to fly under the radar. When you do have to strike, it must be like the thunderbolt and in such a way that isn't traced back to your people. The hour is late, and the position of Americans is perilous. There can be no mistakes and where there are mistakes made, have the heroism to take the fall for your people, to not cause them further injury.

All the traditional ways of making it are almost all off the table. They were established by our ancestors, yes, but now they are owned by traitors and enemies. The way forward is breaking free of our dependence on the system. Becoming responsible for ourselves. It's a hard and unforgiving road into the frontier, but it's a path you must travel if you want to win. The enemy wants you weak, it wants you comfortable and dependent. That's how they control you. We have to form our own networks and embrace the wild again. The new frontier.

Through this, we can form a new social cohesion that the enemy won't ever be able to understand. A racial trait of our people is the ability to tame the wilderness. There's a reason why 98% of the history that matters was accomplished by White peoples. Not every race is capable of this. Our ancestors tamed an enormous landmass. Our ancestors made a mighty empire out of the New World. This has been taken from you, but it's in your blood to make one better, stronger.

That is the Great Task before us. There are few among our people who understand what's happened, who understand how mindfucked our people have become. Is this providence for the noble and heroic? You are in a position to reforge the Way of the Fathers. To become a Father yourself. Found a new Patrician Order. Are you up to the task?

The original Roman Patricians, the Fathers, were chosen by Romulus because they helped found Rome. I call upon new

American Patricians to do the same. This book has been a testament of power to what must be done to resurrect the BARBARIC VITALISM of our ancestors. Secure your bloodlines, free your family from the psychological warfare being waged upon them and make yourself a part of a warrior brotherhood. Forge alliances with likeminded groups and retake your country. This all requires work and sacrifice. It ain't all about fighting, you also have to take part in foundation building, acquiring wealth, and power.

Something to remember about Barbaric Vitalism and the Way of the Fathers, is that our ancestors had to fight and there's something that gets activated on the biological level, in the blood, when you partake in physical culture and fighting. No matter where you are in this life, you must strive to be a warrior. If you're young, take up my friend Bane's recommendation to join the national guard infantry. If you're past that point, do what you can to become a fighter and instill this mentality into your sons. Martial excellence must be the goal of every American. It's used to be said that we were born with gun in hand. War is always changing, we cannot be exactly like our ancestors who were Hoplites, Legionaries, Knights, Soldiers, or Frontiersmen. Modern soldering has certain requirements, and you must make yourself better at it than our enemies.

Be a man of dogged discipline. Let the masses engage in whatever degeneracy is the flavor of the month. Devote yourself to the way of the Warrior. Devote yourself to God and a new Warrior Religion. Set your sights on the Golden Path. Become a religious fanatic who can see the bigger picture and the Golden Path of God hidden by civilization. Do all this and you will bring VITALITY back to our race.

A man of vitality acts on instincts. He isn't held back by rationale or facts or logic. Instinct is truer than any of that. You cannot outsmart thousands of years of surviving in nature. To act on instinct is to once again become Spengler's culture man and when you can do this, you will gain the potential to make your own culture. To become truly SOVEREIGN.

Printed in Great Britain
by Amazon

41369284R10103